Rumi Teaching

A Guide to Self-Discovery and Personal Growth

Dr. Farid Mostamand

Dedicated to My Wife, Rokshana

Table of Contents

Rumi's Teachings on True Happiness

Rumi, the great poet, and philosopher, offers profound insights into the nature of true happiness and the path to its attainment. Rooted in the core concepts of the illusionary self, *Mazehab Ishq* (the religion of Love), and the interconnectedness of human and divine love, his teachings provide a roadmap for transcending the limitations of the illusionary self and establishing a profound connection with the source. (Beloved, Universal Consciousness)

In this chapter, we delve into the depths of Rumi's teachings on true happiness and explore the transformative power of love. We begin by examining the illusionary self, which Rumi emphasizes as the primary obstacle to experiencing genuine fulfillment.

Transcending the Illusionary Self:

Rumi's teachings emphasize the importance of transcending the illusionary self to establish a profound connection with our ultimate source, beloved or universal consciousness. According to Rumi, true happiness remains elusive until we liberate ourselves from the confines of this Illusionary prison. The illusionary self can be likened to a shell that obscures our true essence, much like a pearl. We must break free from this restrictive shell to live authentically and unite with the source.

Life presents a remarkable battle between our true selves and the illusionary personas we construct. Unless we triumph over the illusionary self, we remain imprisoned in a state of unhappiness, sadness, and dissatisfaction. A lingering sense of loneliness and emptiness persists even when surrounded by loved ones. Deep within us, we sense that something crucial is missing, yet we struggle to define it. Discovering the missing piece necessitates connecting with our true selves and living harmoniously with our authentic being. However, before embarking on this transformative journey, it is crucial to understand the illusionary and authentic selves clearly. We can establish that connection and attain true happiness by dismantling the illusionary self.

The Nature of the Illusionary Self:

The illusionary self comprises of complex elements, including our past and present experiences, real and imagined images, the influence of others, cultural and religious conditioning, upbringing, and, most significantly, our thoughts and emotions. Some psychologists propose that our voices represent the ego responsible for constructing and upholding the illusionary self. This construct takes root during childhood and solidifies within us, eventually becoming our perceived identity. As adults, we cling to this illusionary reality, rejecting anything that challenges its constraints.

Over time, this imaginary construct becomes our unquestioned belief system, making it incredibly challenging to break free from the self-imposed prison we have constructed. We remain trapped, believing that departing from this Illusionary state would defy societal norms and endanger our safety, even though no physical barriers confine us. The illusionary self manipulates our beliefs and fears, ensuring its stronghold over us, thereby perpetuating our captivity.

The illusionary self mirrors our thoughts, emotions, and memories, whether real or unreal. It engenders our suffering and unhappiness. As the self is a blend of reality and imagination, our sorrows and sadness may be genuine or merely products of our thoughts and emotions.

At birth, we enter the world with a clean slate, unburdened by the illusionary self. However, as we grow and interact with our environment, this Illusionary construct becomes our primary instructor and guide. It thrives on competition, comparison, conflict, and the pursuit of superiority over others. The Illusionary self is highly sensitive, easily wounded, and becomes unhappy when circumstances fail to align with its desires.

The Illusionary self becomes the sole reality we know throughout our lives. We find solace and security within this familiar realm, hesitant to venture into the unknown. Rumi referred to this Illusionary self as the "*Nafs*," the selfish self, a prison without tangible walls. He regarded it as humanity's greatest adversary.

The authenticity of the Illusionary self arises from the mind's capacity to make it real for us. However, its reality dissipates once we comprehend that it is merely a narrative constructed from our thoughts, emotions, and memories. Armed with this understanding, we journey toward our true selves, a realm of inner divinity and true happiness.

Our dualistic perception gives rise to the Illusionary self, shaping a pseudo-reality from memories that appear and feel genuine to us. Dismantling this dualistic perception marks the demise of the Illusionary self, a concept known as "*Fana*" in Rumi's teachings.

Stuck in the Loop of Memory:

To illustrate the workings of the Illusionary self, consider this example: Imagine visiting a picturesque mountain village in Switzerland for the first time. The awe-inspiring beauty of the snow-capped peaks and the refreshing air leave you speechless, as your mind lacks preconceived notions or prior experiences to categorize and interpret this scene.

Subsequent visits, however, fail to evoke the same sense of wonder. This occurs because, on your initial visit, your mind categorized the experience, creating a story that became etched in your memory. During subsequent visits, instead of directly experiencing the present moment, you merely replay a mental movie crafted from your initial encounter—a projection of the Illusionary self.

Suppose your first visit transpired during winter, while your subsequent visit occurred in spring when the village transformed into a verdant landscape adorned with blooming wildflowers. Rather than immersing yourself in the present, your Illusionary self-retrieves memories from your first visit, replaying them and denying you the opportunity to embrace the freshness of the current experience. Consequently, the subsequent visit lacks the excitement and novelty of the initial encounter.

This example illustrates the Illusionary nature of the self, underscoring the realization that our perceptions and experiences are not inherently genuine.

Embracing the Present Moment:

This awareness serves as a crucial starting point on the path toward the religion of love, guiding us to reconnect with our true selves. By doing so, we relinquish the passive role of reliving recorded memories and become active participants in the present moment. True happiness and inner peace reside in the present, not the past. Therefore, choosing to live solely within the confines of the Illusionary self deprives us of genuine fulfillment. To embark on a path toward authentic existence, we must initiate the journey of destroying the Illusionary self and reconnecting with our true selves.

"When you die, you will receive another life.

This life is transient and not everlasting.

Love is the life-giving nectar of mortality.

This is why we call it the water of life.

Cone into this source of life and see,

That every drop is an ocean by itself."

"When you die" here, Rumi refers to the death of the illusionary self (*Fana*). Another life is a metaphor that replaces the illusionary self to describe the true self. Love is the only vehicle that takes us from one place to another. Even though we are a drop of the ocean, we have all the essence of the ocean.

Mazehab Ishq:

Mazehab Ishq, translated as the religion of Love, is the path that Rumi advocates for connecting with the beloved and attaining spiritual enlightenment. It is a direct and personal approach to spirituality that emphasizes the importance of love over strict religious rules and dogmas. *Mazehab Ishq* invites individuals to embark on a transformative journey of self-discovery and divine connection through love. Rumi teaches that by cultivating love in our hearts and embracing it as the guiding principle, we can navigate the complexities of existence and reunite with the source.

Mazehab Ishq, the religion of Love, is the path Rumi offers, urging individuals to prioritize love as the guiding principle in their lives. Through the cultivation of love, both human and divine, we can embark on a transformative journey toward spiritual awakening and reconnect with our true essence.

"I   declare   the   religion   of   Love,
Love is my only faith."

Rumi's teaching on The Transformative Power of Love:

Rumi distinguishes between divine Love (*Ishq Haqiqi*) and human love (*Ishq Mojazi*), highlighting their unique while emphasizing their interconnectedness. Divine Love, *Ishq Haqiqi,* represents the highest form of love that leads to unity with the beloved and provides a pathway to the divine source. It is a love that transcends the physical realm's limitations and encompasses our being's spiritual essence. On the other hand, human love, *Ishq Mojazi,* refers to the love experienced in human relationships and connections. Rumi asserts that divine Love and human love travel the same pathway of *Mazehab Ishq* and share similar qualities of mystical love. He teaches that when nurtured and cultivated, genuine, authentic human love can serve as a steppingstone toward experiencing and understanding the depth of divine Love.

Love is a spiritual connection beyond human interaction's physical or appearance-based aspects. It delves into the depths of the soul, seeking a profound and lasting bond. Rumi emphasizes that love cannot be confined to superficial qualities such as physical attractiveness or lust, as these aspects are fleeting and transitory. True mystic love transcends the transient nature of the physical world and endures even in the face of challenges and impermanence.

Sacrifice, Commitment, and Courage in Rumi's Teachings:

Love, the extraordinary force that transcends boundaries and touches the depths of our spirits, encompasses qualities that shape our relationships and spiritual journeys. Within the teachings of Rumi, we discover four essential aspects of love: sacrifice, commitment, courage, and suffering. These virtues illuminate a deeper connection with us, others, and the divine.

Sacrifice is a fundamental characteristic of love that Rumi highlights in his teachings. According to Rumi, love teaches us the art of selflessness and the willingness to sacrifice our self-interest and ego. It is through sacrifice that love reaches its highest expression and transformative power. When we let go of our desires, expectations, and attachments, we create space for love to flourish and connect us to something greater than ourselves. This act of sacrifice is not one of deprivation or loss but an opportunity for growth and expansion of the heart.

"If you're unwilling to undress, don't enter the stream of the truth."

Rumi beautifully expresses this idea through the metaphor of undressing oneself. Love demands that we metaphorically undress our illusions, masks, and barriers to enter the realm of our true selves. By shedding our false identities and embracing vulnerability, we open ourselves to the transformative power of love. Through this undressing, we reveal our authentic essence, paving the way for a deep and meaningful connection with the beloved.

Another characteristic of love that Rumi emphasizes is commitment. Love requires unwavering commitment and dedication to the beloved. It is not an emotion or a passing feeling but a steadfast devotion that endures through all circumstances. Rumi compares true lovers to lotus leaves that remain untainted by the mud surrounding them. They remain committed to their love, regardless of external influences or temptations. This commitment stems from the deep understanding that love is not just an emotional bond but a spiritual journey that requires steadfastness and perseverance.

Courage is also an essential aspect of love, according to Rumi. Love demands courage because it entails giving without expecting anything and willing to lose oneself. Rumi describes love as being like a butterfly that offers its life to the flame of a candle without asking for anything in return. It requires the courage to let go of personal desires and attachments, allowing love to flow freely and unconditionally. This courageous act of surrender will enable us to transcend the limitations of the ego and experience the profound unity that love offers.

Love is about pain and suffering. The lover must tolerate the pain of separation until one is purified enough to join the beloved throughout the path of the religion of love.

"Love is best when it comes with anguish,

In our town, we don't call you a lover,

If you cannot endure the pain of love.

Welcome the love this way in your soul,

And watch your soul fly away with ecstasy."

Unity is a central theme in Rumi's teachings on love. Love is not just a connection between individuals but a force that seeks unity and harmony in all aspects of existence. Rumi believes that love is the very cause of creation itself, and without it, the universe would cease to exist. Love is the thread that weaves together the fabric of the cosmos, transcending boundaries and divisions. It inspires us to see the best in others and fosters a sense of unity and harmony, even among those who may hold different beliefs or lifestyles.

"A life without love is of no benefit.
Love is the water of life.
Drink it down with heart and soul."

"With life as short as half-taken breath,
Don't plant anything but love."

Through these characteristics of love—sacrifice, commitment, courage, and suffering —Rumi provides a roadmap for experiencing the transformative power of love in our lives. By embracing love in its most genuine and profound sense, we can cultivate a deeper connection with ourselves, others, and the divine. Love becomes a catalyst for our spiritual growth and an expression of our highest potential. As Rumi beautifully articulates, love is not merely something to be described or understood; it is something to be felt and experienced at the core of our being.

Rumi's perspective on love transcends the boundaries of human perception, as he envisions it as the force that sustains the entire universe. In Rumi's worldview, love is not merely an abstract concept or a fleeting emotion; it is the cosmic energy that fuels the dance of existence itself. The analogy he employs to describe this cosmic dance is waves propelling a wheel's turning. Just as waves ripple through the vast expanse of an ocean, love reverberates through the fabric of the cosmos, setting in motion the intricate interplay of life and creation.

Rumi considers Love to be the force that sustains the entire universe.

"The waves of Love turn the wheel of the universe."

For Rumi, the significance of love lies in its capacity to breathe life into the seemingly ordinary and mundane. Without love, the world would be a minuscule, inconspicuous entity devoid of meaning or purpose. Rumi perceives love as the primal energy that ignited the cataclysmic event known as the big bang—the moment that birthed the vast expanse of the universe. In this sense, love becomes the fundamental impetus behind the creation and sustenance of the cosmos as we know it.

Without love, the world would be a tiny nonvisible matter. Rumi sees Love as the force that created the universe in this sense. In other words, in the eye of Rumi, Love is that mysterious energy that made the big bang.

Rumi's teachings on returning to the source through the religion of Love offer profound insights and guidance for our spiritual journeys. Throughout this chapter, we have explored vital concepts such as the illusionary self, divine Love, *Mazehab Ishq*, and the interconnectedness of human and divine love. These teachings invite us to embark on a transformative path of self-discovery and divine connection.

Rumi's emphasis on recognizing and dismantling the illusionary self reminds us to let go of false identities and attachments that hinder our spiritual growth. By shedding these illusions, we create space for the emergence of our true selves and open the doors to unity with the beloved.

Practically applying Rumi's teachings involves reflecting on our own lives and relationships. It requires cultivating love within us and extending it to others, breaking down the barriers that separate us from unity with the beloved. By nurturing love as a guiding force, we can transform our perspectives, enhance our connections, and experience the divine within and around us.

As we continue our spiritual journeys, let us reflect on the teachings of Rumi and embrace the transformative power of love. Let us be mindful of the illusionary self and work towards its dissolution. Let us embody the qualities of love and commit ourselves to unity with the beloved.

Rumi said, "*With life as short as half-taken breath, don't plant anything but love.*"

So, let us sow the seeds of love in our hearts and nurture them with compassion, kindness, and understanding. By doing so, we can return to the source through love and experience the fulfillment and everlasting joy that unity with the beloved brings.

May the wisdom of Rumi's teachings guide us in embracing love as the guiding light in our lives and lead us on a profound journey of self-discovery and divine connection.

"I practice the religion of love.
My faith and my religion are love
My mother is love.
My prophet is love.
My God is love,
I am a child of love,
I have come to speak of nothing ...
But love!"

Rumi intricately weaves these concepts of the illusionary self, Love, *Mazehab Ishq*, and *Ishq Haqiqi/Ishq Mojazi* into his teachings, forming the overarching theme of returning to the source through love. Rumi asserts that the illusionary self, with its attachments, ego, and false identities, keeps us separate from the beloved and hinders our connection with the divine.

By recognizing and dismantling this illusionary self, we create space for the emergence of divine Love within us, which leads to unity with the source and true happiness.

The Universal Essence of Rumi's teaching:

Rumi's journey led him to question and transcend the confines of organized religion, mainly as he delved deeper into his spiritual connection with the beloved. While Rumi remained deeply rooted in his Islamic faith throughout his life, his understanding of God and spirituality expanded beyond the boundaries of religious dogmas and institutions.

Rumi's encounters and profound friendship with Shams Tabrizi, a wandering mystic and spiritual guide, significantly shaped his evolving views on organized religion. Shams ignited within Rumi a longing for a direct and unmediated experience of the divine. This experience led Rumi to shift his focus from the external rituals and practices of religion to the internal realm of the heart.

Rumi believed that true spirituality and the path to the divine lay within the depths of the individual's being. He saw organized religion, emphasizing rules, rituals, and dogmas, as potential barriers that could obstruct the direct experience of divine love. Rumi's spiritual journey led him to question the established religious structures and how they often limited individuals' access to God.

"I looked in temples, churches, and mosques. But I found the Divine within my heart."

His poems and teachings reflect his belief that God is not confined to any books, place, or religious tradition. Instead, Rumi emphasized that God's essence resides within individuals' hearts. He saw the heart as the sacred temple where we can intimately experience the divine. Rumi believed that the religion of love, *Ishq*, is the true pathway to God, enabling individuals to reunite with the beloved.

Rumi's perspective on organized religion did not reject spirituality or religious principles. Instead, it was a call for a deeper, more personal connection with the divine, unencumbered by the limitations imposed by human constructs. Rumi believed that the true essence of religion lies in the unity of all beings and the pursuit of love, compassion, and spiritual enlightenment.

Rumi's teachings emphasize that love and spiritual awakening transcend religious boundaries and are available to anyone who seeks the truth and the divine connection within their hearts.

While Rumi's views on religion transformed after he met Shams, we cannot separate Rumi from his core belief inspired by his religion, which is about inclusion, not exclusion.

"I pray in church,

I pray in the temple,

I pray in synagogue,

I pray in the mosque.

I pray to one God."

His poetry is about the mystery of the universe, the imprisonment of the spirit, love, separation, relationships, and his prime message of divinity within. He believed our spirits were united and contained in the universal consciousness before our physical existence. Like other Sufis, Rumi thought we could not understand God if we didn't understand ourselves.

"I lost myself in God, and now God is mine. Don't search for Him in any direction, as He is in my spirit."

Rumi's God within belief is much different from other Muslims who believe in separating God and self. God is the creator of life and the universe and doesn't have anyone like him. He is the only one. He is light without any physical body.

Divinity Within and Organized Religion

The idea of the direct path to God challenges the status quo and is the cause of concern in the established order. Most of the time, the established orders move people away from the union with God with dogma, religious rituals, and self-served interpretation of their holy books. They subvert the spiritual journey for many believers and followers of a specific religion.

Control is one of the main reasons for the establishment to deprive people of direct communication with God. They put an obstacle on the road that only they can remove to make our connection with God possible. They set up rules and guidelines to only benefit the established, organized religion. They force the follower to do this and not do that if they want union with God. God does not create an obstacle to unite with him. Religious leaders create obstacles for their followers to run to them for help removing the barrier. They have more control when there is more obstacle to God's unification. They make the connection with God so tricky that the follower flocks to them for direction and guidance.

Theologian and social activist Abraham Heschel summarizes the establishment's power: "Religion becomes sinful when it begins to advocate the segregation of God, to forget that the true sanctuary has no walls. Religion has always suffered from the tendency to become an end, to seclude the holy, parochial, self-indulging, and self-seeking. It has often done more to canonize prejudices than to wrestle for truth. To petrify the sacred than to sanctify the secular. Yet the task of religion is to be a challenge to stabilizing values."

Even all the holy books clearly state that God is everywhere and accessible to you. But the establishment is trying to obscure the simple message of how easy it is to unite and talk to God. They lose control if they give the actual message in all holy books.

Bible says, *"the kingdom of God within."*

Quran also says, *"God is closer to you than your jugular artery."*

"My beloved, you are closer to me than myself; you shine through my eyes."

Suppose we want to remove the veil and be in direct union with God. In that case, we need to emphasize love over rules and laws put forward by organized religion to prevent us from communicating with God directly and without an intermediary. If religions want to direct us toward the union with God, they should point us in the direction of our hearts on the pathway of love, not the pathway of obstacles with rituals, rules, and guidelines.

Religion should be transformative, not emphasizing loyalty to a group or claiming superiority over other groups. *"Whatever purifies you is the right road. I will try not to define it."*

"I got into the Muslim Mosque
And the Jewish synagogue,
And the Christian church,
And I see one altar."

"I searched everywhere,
To find a gift to bring you.
Nothing seemed right.

What is the point of bringing gold to
The gold mine, or water to the sea.

Everything I came up with was like
Taking spices to the Orient.

It is not good giving my heart and my
Spirit because you already have these.
So I brought you a mirror.

Look at yourself and remember me."

Organized religions should be the messengers of
God's message, not the message itself.

Embracing Rumi's Virtues

"In generosity and helping others be like the river,

in compassion and grace be like the sun,

in concealing others' faults be like the night,

in anger and fury be like the dead,

in modesty and humility be like the soil,

in tolerance be like the ocean,

either you appear as you are or be as you appear."

Rumi's teachings encompass many virtues he encouraged his followers to cultivate daily. These virtues include tolerance, modesty, humility, generosity, compassion, and concealing others' faults. Rumi guided how individuals can embody these virtues through his poetry and wisdom to lead a virtuous and meaningful life.

Tolerance was a critical virtue that Rumi emphasized. He encouraged his followers to cultivate an attitude of acceptance and open-mindedness towards others, regardless of their beliefs, backgrounds, and race. Rumi believed tolerance was essential for understanding, harmony, and unity among diverse individuals and communities.

He said, *"Be like the sun in tolerance and generosity. Like the night in covering others' faults. Like a river in compassion and grace."*

Modesty and humility were virtues that Rumi valued deeply. He urged his followers to adopt a modest and humble demeanor, recognizing that true greatness lies not in self-aggrandizement but in selflessness and service to others. Rumi taught that genuine humility is an expression of inner strength and wisdom.

He said, "*In modesty and humility, be like the soil.*" By embodying humility, individuals can connect with others on a deeper level and foster genuine relationships based on mutual respect and humility.

Generosity was another virtue that Rumi emphasized. He encouraged individuals to be generous in their actions, thoughts, and words. Rumi believed that generosity is not limited to material possessions but extends to offering others kindness, love, and support.

He said, "*In generosity and helping others, be like the river.*"

Rumi taught that through acts of generosity, individuals can create a positive impact on the lives of others and foster a sense of abundance and interconnectedness.

Compassion was at the heart of Rumi's teachings. He urged his followers to cultivate a compassionate attitude towards all beings, showing empathy and kindness even in adversity. Rumi believed compassion is a transformative force that heals wounds, brings solace, and fosters a sense of unity.

He said, "*In compassion and grace, be like the sun.*"

Rumi taught that through acts of compassion, individuals can alleviate suffering and contribute to the well-being of others, creating a more compassionate and empathetic society.

Concealing others' faults was a virtue that Rumi emphasized as well. He encouraged his followers to refrain from judgment and gossip and instead focus on recognizing the inherent goodness in others. Rumi believed concealing others' faults nurtures a spirit of understanding, forgiveness, and harmony.

He said, "*In concealing others' faults, be like the night.*"

Rumi taught that by embracing this virtue, individuals can create a supportive and uplifting community where people feel safe and accepted.

These virtues advocated by Rumi remain relevant and applicable in the twenty-first century. In a world that can often be divisive and polarized, Rumi's teachings on virtues provide a timeless blueprint for building harmonious relationships and fostering a more compassionate society. The principles of tolerance, modesty, humility, generosity, compassion, and concealing others' faults offer practical guidance for navigating the complexities of modern life.

By incorporating these virtues into our daily lives, we can cultivate a more inclusive and empathetic mindset, fostering understanding and respect for diverse perspectives. These virtues enable us to transcend barriers, bridge divides, and create meaningful connections with others. Rumi's wisdom reminds us that by embodying these virtues, we have the power to contribute to a more harmonious and compassionate world where individuals can thrive and experience genuine fulfillment.

In *Manaqib*, Rumi's advice to his son Sultan Baha al-Din Walad,

> *Baha al-Din!*
>
> *If you want to live in Paradise forever, be friends with all and hold malice towards none.*
>
> *Do not ask for too much.*
>
> *Do not think that you are more important than anyone.*
>
> *Be soft, like wax, not sharp like a needle.*
>
> *If you want no harm, say, teach, and think no evil; if you speak well of somebody, you will always be happy. This happiness is Paradise.*
>
> *If you speak ill of someone, you will always be unhappy. This sadness is hell. When you talk of your friends, your inner garden, rich with roses, will bloom.*

When you speak of your enemies, your inner garden fills with thorns, and you become stressed and exhausted.

A Journey of Spiritual Awakening

In the realm of mystic poetry, there exists an extraordinary tale of two souls destined to intertwine—a story that would shape the life and work of one of history's most celebrated poets, Rumi. At the heart of this tale lies the transformative encounter between Rumi, and Shams Tabrizi, a pragmatic mystic saint. Their meeting ignited a creative and spiritual fire within Rumi that burned with an intensity unmatched by any other experience in his life.

Rumi, renowned for his intellectual prowess, discovered that his scholarly pursuits alone could not quench the thirst of his restless spirit. It was through his encounter with Shams, a spiritual wanderer on a quest for a worthy student, that Rumi's journey took an unexpected turn. Their bond transcended societal expectations and social classes, pushing the boundaries of convention in a highly structured society.

Rumi and Shams embarked on a journey of friendship that delved deep into the realms of spirituality, love, and self-discovery. Their conversations, known as "*Sohbet*," became the foundation upon which Rumi's mystical teachings would flourish. Through their exchange of wisdom, Rumi learned to seek God within the confines of religious dogmas and the depths of his being.

The impact of Shams on Rumi's life and work was profound and far-reaching. Once known for his intellectual pursuits, Rumi became an ecstatic mystic guided by the religion of love. His poetry, infused with the essence of divine inspiration, resonated with seekers of truth across the ages. The depth of Rumi's spiritual transformation and his ability to articulate the ineffable mysteries of the heart can be traced back to the mystical bond he shared with Shams.

The exact details of Rumi and Shams Tabrizi's first encounter may forever remain shrouded in the mists of time. Various versions of this momentous event have been passed down through the ages, each carrying its poetic allure. While historical validation may elude us, what remains undeniable is the profound impact of their meeting on the trajectory of Rumi's life and spiritual journey.

One such story recounts how Rumi, known for his penchant for engaging with people from all walks of life, would often spend afternoons in the company of farmers, merchants, and ordinary townspeople. In this humble setting, sitting outside his friend Zarkoob's shop, Rumi immersed himself in everyday life's vibrant tapestry. Little did he know that fate had something extraordinary in store for him on this seemingly ordinary day.

A figure caught his attention as Rumi sat on his wooden stool, engrossed in conversation with those around him. Shams Tabrizi, a wandering dervish, passed by, capturing Rumi's curiosity. Without hesitation, Rumi rose from his seat and approached the enigmatic figure, compelled by an irresistible force that drew them together.

Looking intently into Shams' eyes, Rumi asked a simple yet profound question, "Are you a traveler?" Shams, the epitome of mystical wisdom, halted in his tracks, fixing his gaze upon Rumi. In a voice brimming with spiritual depth, he replied, "No, my place is placeless, and every town is my town."

At that moment, Rumi felt a surge of recognition and an inexplicable connection with this mysterious wanderer. Sensing extraordinary wisdom within Shams, Rumi invited him to join him at his friend's shop, where they could engage in a "*Sohbet*" - a profound conversation that would begin an extraordinary bond.

Legend has it that Rumi tested Shams, seeking to delve deeper into mystic knowledge. Their dialogue, echoing through the annals of time, resonates with timeless wisdom.

Rumi asked, "What is religion?"

Shams responded, "Looking for God outside yourself."

Rumi, intrigued, inquired further, "And what is spirituality?"

Shams replied, "Looking for God inside of you."

Rumi's understanding expanded with each question and answer, and his heart opened wider to the truths revealed in their exchange.

Their dialogue continued to unravel the secrets of existence.

Rumi posed the question, "What is wisdom?"

Shams replied, "Wisdom is experiential learning."

Rumi, eager to grasp the nuances of knowledge, asked, "Is knowledge the same as wisdom?"

Shams responded gently, "No, knowledge is learned from books and schools, while wisdom emanates from the depths of your being."

Rumi sought Shams' insight into the human experience as the conversation deepened. "What is poison?" he inquired.

Shams answered, "Anything more than our necessity is poison - power, wealth, greed, or ambition."

Thirsting for further enlightenment, Rumi questioned, "And what is fear?"

Shams, ever the sage, replied, "Fear is the non-acceptance of uncertainty. Embrace uncertainty, and it transforms into an adventure."

The exchange continued, illuminating the nature of emotions and their transformative potential.

Rumi asked, "What is envy?"

Shams responded, "Envy is the non-acceptance of the good in others. Embrace their goodness, and it becomes an inspiration."

Rumi probed more profoundly, "And what about anger?"

Shams imparted his wisdom, "Anger dissipates when we accept things beyond our control, transforming into tolerance."

Finally, Rumi sought to understand the nature of hatred. "What is hatred?" he asked.

Shams' profound reply echoed through the depths of Rumi's being, "Hatred is the non-acceptance of a person as they are. Embrace them unconditionally, and it blossoms into love."

Rumi was so impressed by Shams's response that he asked him to come to his house. Shams followed Rumi to his house. The family didn't think much about a strange dervish coming to their house. In the past, Rumi brought some travelers home who didn't have a place to stay in the town. That night they continued their conversation past midnight. In the morning, Rumi asked Shams to spend a few more days with him. The family and friends become uncomfortable with having a commoner in their house, taking much of Rumi's time. A month passed, and Shams still lived in Rumi's house. The son told his dad it was hurting his reputation by allowing Shams to live in their house. The family noticed they spent many nights together without any sleep.

Gradually the tension between Shams and Rumi's family and friends reached a boiling point. There was no place for Shams in Rumi's social circle. They were the two extremes ends of the social class coming together in a highly structured society. Rumi was a highly regarded scholar who taught the country's ruler. Despite all the warnings from his family and friend, Rumi kept Shams in his house for more than two years and spent most of the night conversing (*Sohbet)* with Shams.

But after constant threats, Shams was forced to leave Konya. Rumi was devastated after Shams left Konya. He started searching for Shams and assigned many people to find him. He soon received the news that shams were spotted in Damascus (in today's Syria). He sent his eldest son Sultan Walad to locate and bring back Shams. Sultan Walad found him and begged him to return. Sultan Walad put Shams on a horse and brought him back to Konya.

Even the family, friends, and townspeople were unhappy about Shams's return, but they wanted their master and spiritual leader, Rumi, to be happy. Rumi fell sick after Shams disappeared.

This time Rumi didn't want to lose Shams again. He married his stepdaughter, Kimia, to Shams. Shams fell in love for the first time in his life. Kimia died a few years after her marriage to Shams, which ended Shams and Rumi's relationship.

There are Rumors of what happened to Shams, but no historical account exists to confirm it. Some believed that Shams left in the middle of the night, continued his life as a wanderer spiritual Darwish, and died a few years after leaving Konya.

Another rumor is that Shams was killed by Rumi's youngest son and Kimia's brother, and his body was thrown in a well. Rumi couldn't accept that Shams was dead. He wrote about Shams's disappearance in Divan-e Shams.

"Who says that the eternal Shams has died?

Who says that the sun of hope has died?"

Shams in Farsi means sun. Later sun became his favorite word used in most of his poetry. Rumi's sickness and heartbreak were evident after Shams disappeared. This heartbreak changed Rumi forever and made him the love mystic poet we know today. There are stories of Rumi's sickness after the shams disappeared. He didn't leave home for months. He lost himself when he was with Shams and found himself when he lost Shams. After the heartbreak, Rumi entered the world of divinity within and produced the most epic enchanting mystic poetry ever written. He lost Shams, but he found himself.

Rumi named his first epic book, shams collection (*Divan-i Kebir*, also known as Divan I Shams), after his mentor, shams Tabrizi.

"Sorrow prepares you for happiness.
It violently sweeps everything out of your house,
so that new joy can find space to enter.
It shakes the yellow leaves from the bough of your heart,
so that fresh, green leaves can grow in their place.

It pulls up the rotten roots,
so that new roots hidden beneath have room to grow.
Whatever sorrow shakes from your heart,
far better things will take their place."

After Shams's encounter, Rumi turned to the religion of love and knew it was the only pathway connecting him to his beloved. After Shams's meeting, Rumi's worldview turned upside down. He became more of a mystical and spiritual person than a religious man. He relied more on his heart than his head. He produced his best poetry after meeting and spending time with Shams. Shams changed Rumi's world and inspired him to look deep inside his heart for true wisdom.

"Your face is like the sun, O Shamsuddin,
With which the hearts are wandering Like clouds!"

Shams put fire in Rumi's imagination and transformed him from an Islamic scholar to an ecstatic Mystic. Shams helped Rumi know his heart in a way never known to him. After Shams, whatever Rumi did in his life, he did it from his heart and became the poet of the hearts.

"The sun (Shams) of Tabriz is an ultimate light,
A sun, one of the beams of God.
When we heard praise of the "Sun of Tabriz,"
The sun of fourth Heaven bowed its head."

Sufism: Exploring the Mystic Path of the Heart

To understand Rumi's teaching, we need to understand Sufism. Rumi was a mystic Sufi.

Sufism, an ancient mystical tradition within Islam, offers a unique and profound approach to spirituality. Rooted in the pursuit of divine love and knowledge, Sufism emphasizes the direct personal experience of the divine, seeking to establish a deep connection with the source of all existence.

The Essence of Sufism:

Sufism is characterized by its focus on experiential spirituality and cultivating a deep, intimate connection with the divine. Sufis seek to attain a state of spiritual enlightenment and union with the beloved (God) through practices such as meditation, remembrance (zikr), contemplation, and ecstatic devotion (Sama). At the core of Sufism lies the belief that the human soul yearns for a reunion with its divine origin, which is realized through the purification of the heart.

Sufism strongly emphasizes the concept of tawhid, the oneness of God, and the recognition that all existence emanates from a single divine source. Sufis perceive the universe as a manifestation of divine love and view every aspect of creation as a reflection of divine attributes. They seek to transcend the limitations of the material world and experience the underlying spiritual reality that permeates all things.

Love as the Central Theme:

Human and divine love is a central theme in Sufism and Rumi's teachings. Sufis perceive love as the fundamental force that binds the universe and the key to spiritual awakening. Rumi's poetry abounds with metaphors and imagery depicting love's transformative power. Through his verses, he invites individuals to embark on a journey of self-discovery, where the heart becomes the gateway to divine connection.

Whirling Dervishes: Ecstasy and Remembrance:

One of the most iconic aspects of Sufism is the practice of the whirling dance, often associated with the Mevlevi Order founded by Rumi's followers. Known as the *Sama*, the whirling dervishes perform this ecstatic dance as a form of remembrance and spiritual communion with the divine. The swirling motion represents the rotation of the planets, embodying the idea of cosmic harmony and unity.

Teachings and Principles:

Sufism encompasses many teachings and principles that guide its practitioners toward spiritual transformation. Fundamental principles include the cultivation of humility, detachment from worldly attachments, and the development of ethical conduct and compassion. Sufis often emphasize the importance of a spiritual guide or teacher (*Murshid*) who provides guidance and support on the journey toward self-realization.

Universal Appeal of Sufism:

While Sufism originated within the Islamic tradition, its teachings, and practices have transcended religious and cultural boundaries. Sufi concepts such as divine love, unity, and the inward journey of the soul resonate with individuals from various backgrounds and belief systems. Sufi poetry, including Rumi's verses, has been translated into numerous languages and continues to inspire seekers of truth worldwide.

Sufism, the mystical path within Islam, offers a profound approach to spirituality, emphasizing the direct personal experience of the divine and the cultivation of love and knowledge. Rumi, as a Sufi poet and spiritual master, exemplifies the essence of Sufism through his teachings on divine love, the transformative power of the heart, and the journey of the spirit. With its universal appeal and timeless wisdom, Sufism continues to serve as a guiding light for those seeking spiritual enlightenment and a deeper connection with the divine.

Unveiling the True Self in Rumi's Teachings

The prime message of Rumi revolves around recognizing the divinity within. Rumi emphasizes that the true self is an integral part of the whole, interconnected with the source of existence. Understanding and knowing this divine essence within us is intricately tied to comprehending ourselves. Rumi believed that one could not truly understand God without first understanding oneself. It is crucial to explore and gain mastery over our innate qualities, such as desires and attachments to material possessions, which can hinder our connection with our authentic selves.

Rumi beautifully captures this notion of inner divinity when he states, "Don't you know yet? It is your light that lights the universe." This profound realization highlights that the light of our being is not separate from the cosmic light that permeates the universe.

To understand the true nature of self, we must understand the relationship between the part and the whole.

In Sufism, every part has all elements of the whole.

Rumi said, "*You are not just a drop of the ocean; you are the entire ocean in a drop.*"

Rumi reminds us that we are a part of the whole, and our spirit is not separate from the source. Rumi says that for spiritual growth, we do not need anything from the outside; all we need are within us.

Before man's physical existence, all spirits (parts) were united and contained in Universal intelligence (whole, Source). Humans existed in spirituality or consciousness before being placed in a physical body.

Rumi frequently depicts this paradoxical tension between the individual notion of the illusionary self (*Nafs*) and the true self throughout the *Masnavi*. He said, *"You cannot love God without loving yourself."*

"I said to God; I will not die,

Before I know you.

God replied, "he who

knows me never dies."

Rumi said that there is an inherent sadness in the spirit of everyone. Our separation from the source causes this sadness. We are heartbroken about being separated from the source. We cannot reach true happiness if we cannot connect with the source (whole, Universal intelligence, spirit, God).

One of the core philosophies of Rumi and Sufism is the desire to return to the source. This separation of loneliness creates fear, anxiety, and insecurity. The true sense of happiness and wisdom is in joining with the source. We are not secure and safe when we are separated from our essence, like a drop of water from the ocean; soon, it evaporates and is annihilated if it does not return to the safety of the sea.

Like countless other Sufis, Rumi believed that knowledge of God is intimately tied to knowledge of the self. Therefore, when considering a term like "self" in Rumi's Sufi tradition, we often refer to something quite specific but simultaneously complex, multifaceted, and elusive. Rumi's notion of (the self) is a non-physical entity that are complex dimensions of the "self."

In this sense, the English term "self" is too broad for what we are dealing with when we examine the works of Rumi when he refers to the "self."

Therefore, when Rumi refers to the self, he often refers to all four parts of the self.

1-Spirit

2-Soul

3-Body

4-Heart

Let us examine each part closely.

Spirit

The soul and spirit are usually interchangeable, but they are different. Sufism believes that the spirit is the true self and the soul is *Nafs* (illusionary self). But this explanation only describes a simplified differentiation between the soul and spirit.

The soul or illusionary self is our mind, thoughts, feelings, emotions, and free will that can do good or evil. God specifically creates the soul for us; there is no other one like it. Once the body is destroyed, the soul dies with it.

The spirit is eternal, ingrained within us since birth. Within ourselves, we hold the essence of the source and its entirety. This aspect of our being constitutes our true self. We have a choice to live in the illusionary world or embrace our genuine essence—the true self and divinity within. The spirit represents a fragment of universal intelligence, integrating into the self with the first breath. It comprises a component of the whole, encompassing all elements within it. This component manifests as the realm of divinity within, surrounding both the true and higher selves.

"You are born of divinity; You have always possessed the divine essence."

This separated part of Universal intelligence becomes the central element of self. This part is infinite and does not change. As the body disappears, the spirit rejoins the source unique to that self (you). If this part (spirit) moves into another body, it becomes the same self (you) minus feeling, thought, desire, and Free will.

Soul

In Rumi Sufism, the soul is *Nafs* (Illusionary self) that contains thoughts, emotions, and free will capable of inciting good or evil.

Neuroscientists believe that the mind or the soul is a physical activity of the brain. So to the scientist, the soul or mind is a manifestation of brain activity. But they have not presented any convincing scientific evidence to prove their theory. They have not identified any part of the brain that contains emotion or feeling, and they have not associated emotion and feeling with the firing of any neuron.

Body

The body is that part of the self that contains the spirit. Rumi and Sufism believe that the spirit separates from the source (Universal intelligence) and gets into the body.

"Don't look at yourself as a body of clay.

See yourself as a mirror, reflecting,

The divine beauty."

The Heart's Intuitive Wisdom: Exploring Rumi's Spiritual Path

Rumi talks about the heart as the center of our spirit. This nonphysical heart is where our emotions and feelings of love exist. When Rumi refers to the heart, he means heart wisdom, the light of divine love, and the center of divinity.

If the world of divinity within is our solar system, the heart intelligence is the sun, the star of our solar system. The planet that is closer to the sun receives intense sun energy. Even by becoming aware of our divinity within, we get some access to the sun (Heart intelligence, divine energy).

Rumi does not talk about the heart as a biological pump. It is a field or metaphor for love and compassion. It is the center of divinity within. It is the sun in our solar system.

Heart-intuitive wisdom is a nonintellectual experience of reality we can feel and access after taking the first step toward the new world of divinity. According to Rumi, heart intelligence and its intuitive wisdom are about the awareness of the divinity within.

Life begins at the center of our hearts. Rumi referred to this awareness as opening one's heart. This awareness is essential for understanding the true meaning of Rumi's mystic poetry. This awareness is like a stair to the roof.

"When you take the first step, the way appears."

In the first step, we become aware of our true selves. Once we are on the top (Enlightenment, higher self), we have reached a total awareness of our divinity within, where we have complete access to the heart's intelligence and intuitive wisdom.

"I searched for him on the Christian cross; he was not there.
I searched the temple of the Hindus,
But I didn't find a trace of Him.

I searched the mountains and the valleys,
But I did not find him anywhere.

I went to Kaaba in Mecca,
but He was not there either...

I questioned the scholars and philosophers,
But he was beyond their understanding .....

Then, I investigated my heart, and it was,
Where he dwelled that I saw Him."

Access to the heart's intuitive wisdom lets us understand a person's intention. This access to the heart's intuitive wisdom enables us to understand people deeper. Once we get to know a person deeper, miscommunication rarely happens, and we make a great connection with other people by simply knowing their true character. Once we intuitively understand a person's real character, our response would be based on understanding a person's real intention and don't create more confusion and disagreement. Therefore, understanding other people on a deeper level improves our relationships with others and brings happiness to our life.

As many might believe, intuitive heart wisdom doesn't mean we get psychic power. It is about awareness; sometimes, that awareness could be the essence of survival. In animal worlds, intuition and wisdom are the essences of their survival.

A bird in Central America flies for a 5000-mile journey a couple of days after he is born and reaches a forest where the blossoms of the trees only last for a couple of weeks. Without getting to these trees and eating the nectar of that tree, they cannot survive for long. For these birds, access to their intuition is their survival.

We can't even imagine what the heart reveals to us once we access its intelligence and intuitive wisdom. Most of the time, this access to our heart's intuitive knowledge improves our relationship with others as we realize that we are the source of a disagreement in a relationship because of our inability to understand that person meaningfully.

This access to heart intelligence or awareness of unspoken words allows us to recognize our faults in many of our relationships that are the source of many destroyed relationships. We are not fully connected to our heart's intuitive wisdom to understand a person's real intention in a relationship of any kind- a love relationship, a son and father relationship, a mother and her children relationship, colleagues, or a friend relationship.

We can't even imagine how the world would be so different if we all were aware of and accessed our heart's wisdom and intuitive power. We would see a world full of love, compassion, empathy, harmony, and peace. Heart wisdom and its intuitive wisdom are the only reality, and Everything else is just an imagination. When we access our heart's wisdom, we sense a feeling that does not recognize time and space.

Rumi refers to heart wisdom and its intuitive wisdom (Energetic heart). But as our knowledge about the physical heart expands, one wonders could the physical heart be a manifestation of the energetic or spiritual heart that Rumi refers to.

For centuries, poets and Philosophers considered the heart the center of wisdom, desire, and emotion. Intuition takes shape in the heart without much involvement from the brain. Heart intuitive wisdom is divine wisdom concerned with direct reality experience transcending intellectual thinking and sensory perception. The knowledge that comes from this experience is heart-intuitive wisdom. They believe optimal reality cannot be the object of reasoning, abstracts, and calculations. Heart-intuitive wisdom is a nonintellectual experience of reality.

"If all the candles in the universe flicker and die.

Don't worry; We have the spark that starts the fire."

Knowledge of the head is intellect and acquired; intuitive knowledge of the heart is divine wisdom, and it is within every one of us, ready to be accessed. Here Rumi talks about the heart's Intelligence and its intuitive knowledge.

There are two types of intelligence: acquired,
As a child, you memorize facts and concepts.
from books and the teachers,
As well as from the sciences.

With such knowledge, you rise in the world.
You get ranked ahead or behind others.
concerning your ability to remember
Information. You stroll with this intelligence,
in and out of fields of knowledge, continually getting more
Marks on your preserving tablets.

There is another type of knowledge, one
They are already completed and preserved inside you.
This is wisdom which
Does not turn yellow or decay.

It doesn't travel from outside to inside,
Through acquired learning.

This knowledge is divine wisdom
From within you, moving out."

Rumi talks about the heart as the center of our spirit. This nonphysical heart is where our feeling of love exists. He believes the heart is the spiritual axis that connects us directly with the beloved. Therefore, the heart must be full of love energy to journey toward the beloved. Rumi also believed that the Heart has intuitive wisdom (heart intelligence, heart wisdom) where much of our life decisions occur. Rumi metaphorically referred to true heart intelligence as "Potential, greatness, and wings."

The Heart's Wisdom and Scientific Discoveries:

Scientific findings, such as Dr. Armor's discovery of the heart's "little brain" in 1991, have shed light on the heart's intricate intelligence beyond its function as a mere pump. The heart's energetic intelligence, often spoken of by poets and philosophers, holds vast potential. While scientists primarily study the physical body and rational knowledge, poets, philosophers, and mystics experience the energetic body and the heart's intuitive wisdom, encompassing the ultimate reality.

Understanding Heart Intelligence:

Heart coherence, the state of harmony between the spiritual heart and our emotions, plays a pivotal role. When love, compassion, and humanity guide our emotions, high-frequency vibrations maintain coherence between the energetic heart and the brain. Incoherence creates stress and hinders access to the heart's wisdom and our true potential.

The Heart's Vital Force and Cellular Memory:

The heart acts as a complex communication center, connecting the mind, body, and cells through an intricate network of nerves, peptides, hormones, immune cells, and an energetic force known as the vital force. This vital force, stored in the energetic heart, sends coded messages to every cell in our body, influencing cellular memory and orchestrating physiological functions. It is the dominant force governing the body's chemical and neurological actions, guiding us intuitively before events unfold.

Expanding Knowledge Through the Physical Heart:

While direct scientific study of the energetic heart remains elusive, understanding the functions of the physical heart expands our knowledge of the heart's intelligence. Recognizing that the physical heart reflects the energetic heart, delving into scientific research on the physical heart illuminates the immense power within our spiritual heart.

Embarking on the Heart's Journey:

The heart's journey begins even before physical existence, with the formation of the embryonic heart cell and its first heartbeat. This heartbeat, a symbol of life's beginning, suggests that consciousness resides in the heart, intimately connected to the universal consciousness. Recent scientific developments confirm the heart's role as a neurological, endocrine, and immune organ, surpassing the brain's functions.

Heart Intelligence and Consciousness:

While Philosophers and scientists debate the heart's role in consciousness, some believe that the spirit is consciousness—a part of the universal consciousness. The heart's intricate functioning, its continuation beyond brain death, and the presence of a tiny brain indicate that consciousness is deeply entwined with the heart's intelligence.

Living a Heart-Centered Life:

Acknowledging the heart's intelligence and intuitive wisdom has transformative potential in our lives. Decisions made by the heart often bring a sense of certainty and inner alignment. As we tap into the heart's wisdom, we unlock boundless happiness, success, and meaning. The heart's power is not a recent discovery but something we have sensed and experienced throughout our lives.

The heart's wisdom, an age-old concept cherished by poets, philosophers, and ancient healers, is now gaining recognition in scientific research. While scientists continue to unravel the mysteries of the heart's intelligence, we can embark on a heart-centered life, tapping into its power to transform ourselves and find purpose and fulfillment. Rumi's journey from relying on his intellect to embracing his heart's intelligence inspires us all.

Vital Force and Heart Intelligence: Unlocking the Essence of Life

Rumi's philosophy encompasses understanding vital force, also known as life force, as the intelligence behind all living things. The energy drives growth, maintains harmony, and orchestrates intricate actions within cells. Exploring the concept of vital force in Rumi's philosophy allows us to grasp the profound wisdom of heart intelligence.

The Search for the Fifth Force:

Scientists have identified four known types of energy: gravity, electromagnetic, strong and weak nuclear forces. However, there is growing recognition that an additional force, an undiscovered energy, is essential for the complex organization and harmony observed in living systems. Many ancient cultures believed in the existence of this force, often associated with innate intelligence or universal consciousness.

The Heart's Electromagnetic Field and Beyond:

The heart's electromagnetic field, discovered in recent decades, suggests that the heart possesses a strong energy field. Could this electromagnetic field express the vital force or heart intelligence? The heart's electromagnetic field may encompass this life force, connecting it to the greater energetic web of existence. (Universal Consciousness.)

The Heart as Storehouse of Vital Force:

A vital force, or life force, is stored and managed within the energetic heart. This force is conveyed to every cell, enabling memory, cognition, and synchronized cellular function. While the physical heart provides oxygen and nutrients to the cells, the energetic heart distributes vital energy for life to flourish. Although we cannot yet measure this force directly, its manifestation within every cell demonstrates its undeniable presence.

Accessing Heart Intelligence:

Accessing the heart's intelligence nourishes our soul and fuels our body for optimal performance. It requires discipline and an understanding of the power residing within us. Techniques aimed at opening our hearts enable us to connect with the heart's intelligence energy, transforming our lives and fostering happiness, health, and prosperity.

The Hidden Signals and Higher Sense Perception:

Scientists and researchers have pondered the existence of hidden signals within the heart, such as those observed in electrocardiograms (ECGs). Could these signals indicate the vital force or the heart's intelligent energy? Dr. Shafica Karagulla's interviews with physicians reveal a recognition of such energy, known as "higher sense perception," without a complete understanding of its nature.

The Heart: Gateway to Optimal Health:

Ancient philosophers such as Aristotle, Hippocrates, and Plato recognized the heart's crucial role in life, acknowledging an innate energy or quality within it. The heart's cells communicate through vibration and pulsation, suggesting a unique energetic connection. Any disruption in the heart's function can disturb the management and flow of vital force, potentially leading to disease.

Embracing Heart Intelligence:

Accepting and acknowledging the existence of the energetic heart as the holder and manager of a vital life force does not necessitate subscribing to any spiritual belief. Although we may be unable to measure this energy directly, we can observe its manifestation in the physiological actions of our bodies. Embracing heart intelligence enables us to tap into this vital force, bringing about optimal health and a profound understanding of the essence of life.

Exploring the concept of vital force and heart intelligence allows us to delve into the wisdom that Rumi conveyed through his philosophy. Recognizing the interconnectedness between the energetic heart, vital force, and the greater fabric of existence offers profound insights into the essence of life. Accessing heart intelligence unlocks the potential for transformation, well-being, and a deeper understanding of our place in the universe.

The Dance of Energy and Matter: Rumi's Insights into the Nature of Existence

In this chapter, we delve into the profound connections between Rumi's philosophy and the nature of the universe. We explore the concept of universal consciousness and the interplay between energy and matter, drawing parallels to Rumi's teachings on the existence and the divine essence within all beings.

"To find the beloved,
You must become the beloved."

The universe is made of energy fields that change from energy to matter and from matter back to energy. The matter is a pocket of energy in the quantum field. This field of energy is continuous throughout the universe without any disturbance. Everything in the universe is a part of this field called universal intelligence or universal consciousness, spirit, or the Source.

Nothing in the universe is gained and lost; they change from one state of being to another. Everything is energy at its core. If it vibrates at a lower frequency, it takes the nature of matter and is visible to the human senses; if it vibrates at a higher frequency, it is in the form of energy and not visible or touchable to the human sense.

"You are born of Divinity.
You have always possessed the Divine essence."

Energy and matter are both sides of the same coin. We don't know if we get the energy or matter side of the coin if we rotate a coin.

According to Einstein, only energy exists, and matter is a slower-moving form of energy.

We cannot see the hummingbird's wings because they vibrate at high frequencies. If we could raise our perception to the same frequency as the frequency of the hummingbird's wing, we could see the hummingbird's wing.

We think of an atom as a matter, but 99.999 percent of an atom is empty space.

Some scientists believe that the universe already existed in the form of energy, and only in some small parts of the universe does the vibration energy slow down and become visible.

Then the reality of the universe can be only an illusion, and the only absolute reality is energy.

Einstein said reality is only an illusion, albeit a very persistent one.

Less than five percent of the universe is known matter. The other seventy-five percent is dark matter and dark energy that we know nothing about. Everything in the universe is in a state of vibrating energy.

There is no separation between a particle's energy and matter states at the subatomic level. According to the quantum field theory, at the subatomic level, a particle could exist as a matter and energy at the same time. If there is no true separation between energy and matter at a subatomic level, then we need to reexamine the nature of our physical world. Are we both simultaneously in the form of energy and matter, and only the matter part of our being is detectable to the human sense?

Everything exists in the field of energy and is connected. Every part has the essence of the whole in the field of oneness.

"We are all connected.

To each other biologically.

To the earth, chemically.

To the rest of the universe atomically."

Some religions and philosophers believe that the universe is a manifestation of God, that shows himself to us in the form of the universe. Others believe that this interconnected consciousness is universal consciousness and the spirit. (The Source)

One way to visualize this concept is to observe the state of water. It can be in the form of liquid, gas, or solid, like ice. Once the water evaporates, it doesn't disappear; it takes the state of a being that we cannot see. It doesn't mean that the drop of water we just saw doesn't exist anymore. Simply it is in the form of energy that we don't see. Based on the law of physics, energy cannot be created or destroyed; it just changes from one state of being to another.

"The string is still one string, even if it is tight in thousand knots."

Matter exists as a lump of energy in the quantum field. Does Rumi compare the string to the field and the knots as quanta or lump of energy? Does he refer to the field as the universal consciousness(string) and us as the knots on the string?

So, if the field is the universal consciousness, we are the knots or the burst of energy showing in the field as the matter when it is observed. Does it mean we are just a lump of energy(knots) in the quantum field if it is not observed?

It is hard to understand the exact intention of Rumi in this poem. Still, it has a surprising correlation and similarity with quantum field theory, as though Rumi explained the entire quantum field theory in this poem.

This universal consciousness exists beyond time and space constraints in an infinite world. So, anything finite cannot be conscious. Therefore, our minds cannot be the source of our consciousness, as most neuroscientists believe.

The universe is a converter of high and low vibrating energy. It doesn't create anything; it just converts an energy frequency's speed from high to low and vice versa.

"don't grief; anything you lose comes in different forms."

Shakespeare

"Everything is connected, like a delicate web.

Ever growing, ever-changing. New silvery strands

Come together every day, and once the strand is formed,

No matter what superficial circumstances

It may sometimes keep you apart, but it is never broken.

You will meet again, perhaps in another lifetime.

The connection is unbreakable,

Lying dormant in your subconscious."

The body and the spirit are the ones; the only difference is the frequency of vibration; the spirit, part of the universal consciousness, vibrates at a higher frequency than our physical body, and therefore the physical body is visible, and the spirit is invisible. The same energy appears and disappears in each other once their vibrational frequency is changed.

"Your spirit and mine are the same; we appear and disappear in each other."

Particles have mass in the quantum field, a lump(quanta) of energy that can appear and disappear in the quantum field.

Rumi's Connection to the Mystical Tradition

Rumi was a mystic Sufi. To understand the depth of Rumi's poetry, we need to know what mysticism is. Rumi expressed his mystical experience through myths, metaphors, symbols, poetic images, similes, and allegories.

"If you don't find me within you,

You will never find me.

Because I have been with you,

From the start of me."

Mysticism emerges from a different religious tradition and is more of a spirituality than the practice of a specific religion. Each Mystic is a branch of religion with distinct beliefs that center around the heart and speak about virtue, love, wisdom, consciousness, and empathy. Mysticism is a direct insight into the nature of reality. They have a different view of the human relationship with God. They believe there is no need for dogma to communicate and reach God.

Mystics denounced organized religion as they felt all religions' bases were identical, but many used it for personal gain and recognition. Mysticism believes that many organized religions have been the source of conflict and war for centuries, as each tries to convince its followers that its way is the right pathway to reaching God.

Mystical faith and tradition believe that all roads end with one God and there is no right or wrong way to reach God through the heart and love, not a religious ritual. They believe God is the universe and accessible to everyone. Mystic believes in man's divinity and reunion with God through the pathway of love.

Mysticism in many religions:

Kabbalists -Jewish Mysticism:
The fundamental truth of the Universe that focuses on connecting with the energy flows through the universe.

Gnosticism- Christian Mysticism

Christian Mysticism believes Christ showed his followers a spiritual path to experience God within themselves. They believe connecting with God should be free of religious dogmas.

Sufism-Islamic Mysticism:

Sufi mysticism is about the awareness of self and the awareness of the heart's intuitive intelligence. In Sufi tradition, emotions start in the heart and move to the head. These emotions are energies that affect our thoughts. The heart is also the center of our intuitive guidance, essential for survival. Conscious heart and refining the heart to reach God are crucial elements of the Sufi tradition. Pure refinement of the heart takes many paths:

*"There are as many paths to God
As there are human breaths."*

Rumi's Poetry and Philosophy: Influencing Thinkers Across Time and Space

Rumi's poetry has resonated with countless individuals, inspiring them to find deeper meaning, spiritual connection, and emotional healing. In this chapter, we will explore how Rumi has inspired artists, writers, religious leaders, politicians, and many others and how his legacy continues influencing and uplifting people today.

1: Artists and Musicians

Artists and musicians one of the most prominent examples of Rumi's influence on the arts is the American singer and songwriter Madonna. She has cited Rumi's poetry as an inspiration for her music and performances.

Madonna, known for her boundary-pushing music and thought-provoking lyrics, has drawn inspiration from Rumi's poetry in several of her songs. Rumi's timeless words have given Madonna a rich tapestry of spiritual and philosophical ideas to explore and incorporate into her music. Madonna has sought to convey profound messages of love, self-discovery, and personal transformation through her songs, drawing parallels with Rumi's teachings.

One notable example of Madonna's connection to Rumi can be seen in her song "Frozen" from the album "Ray of Light." In this reflective and introspective track, Madonna explores themes of self-discovery and the importance of breaking free from the constraints of the ego. The lyrics of "Frozen" resonate with Rumi's emphasis on transcending the illusions of the self and embracing one's true essence.

Rumi's poem "The Guest House" has served as a wellspring of inspiration for many artists, including the renowned band Coldplay.

The Guest House:

"This being human is a guest house.

Every morning a new arrival.

A joy, a depression, a meanness,

some momentary awareness comes

as an unexpected visitor.

Welcome and entertain them all!

Even if they're a crowd of sorrows,

who violently sweep your house,

empty of its furniture,

Still, treat each guest honorably.

He may be clearing you out

for some new delight.

The dark thought, the shame, the malice,

meet them at the door laughing,

and invite them in.

Be grateful for whoever comes,

because each has been sent

as a guide from beyond.

This profound poem, with its metaphorical exploration of emotions and experiences as temporary guests, resonates deeply with Coldplay's music and lyrical themes. Coldplay's songs often delve into the complexities of human emotions, the transient nature of life, and the power of embracing joy and sorrow. Rumi's poem has provided Coldplay with a framework to explore these themes, inspiring them to create music that invites listeners to embrace the ever-changing nature of existence and find solace in the beauty of life's transient moments.

Beyoncé and Jay-Z. The couple has referenced Rumi's work in their music and lyrics, incorporating his themes of love, spirituality, and self-discovery into their artistry.

They were so fond of Rumi that they named their daughter after Rumi.

2: Writers and Poets

Rumi's poetry has also influenced several writers and poets over the years. American poet Coleman Barks is perhaps one of the most well-known translators of Rumi's work, having spent many years studying and translating his poetry. Rumi's poetry has also inspired the work of other poets, such as Mary Oliver and Kahlil Gibran, who have referenced Rumi in several of their poems.

3: Religious Leaders

Rumi was a prominent scholar, poet, and philosopher whose work continued to inspire and influence leaders within the religious community. In addition to Pope Francis, other religious leaders, such as the Dalai Lama and the former Archbishop of Canterbury Rowan Williams, have also been drawn to Rumi's poetry. His message of universal love and spiritual connection speaks to the heart of many faiths, and his work has helped to bridge cultural and religious divides.

Rumi had a profound influence on both Islamic and Western cultures. One of the most exciting connections in this regard is between Rumi and Pope Francis, the current head of the Catholic Church.

In 2016, Pope Francis made headlines when he spoke about Rumi during a speech at the Vatican. The Pope praised Rumi's work and described him as a "guide for millions of Muslims and non-Muslims alike, who seek spiritual and social renewal through his writings."

The Pope quoted Rumi's poetry, saying, *"The wound is the place where the light enters you,"* a famous line from one of Rumi's poems that speaks to the transformative power of pain and suffering.

This is not the first time a Pope has shown an interest in Rumi's work. Pope John Paul II, the head of the Catholic Church from 1978 to 2005, was also known to be a fan of Rumi's poetry. He referred to Rumi as a "spiritual master" and even included one of Rumi's poems in a book he wrote titled "Crossing the Threshold of Hope."

The connection between Rumi and the Popes is notable because it speaks to the ability of Rumi's work to transcend religious and cultural boundaries. Rumi's poetry speaks to human experience universally and timelessly, and his message of love, spirituality, and self-discovery resonates with people of all faiths and backgrounds.

The connection between Rumi and the Popes highlights the enduring impact of Rumi's work on global culture and spirituality. Despite the differences between the Islamic and Catholic traditions, Rumi's poetry has bridged these divides, bringing people of all faiths together under a shared message of love and understanding. Rumi's legacy as a spiritual guide and poetic master will continue to inspire and uplift future generations.

4: Politicians

Even politicians have been moved by Rumi's poetry. Former U.S. President Obama referenced Rumi in several speeches, including his 2013 inauguration address.

Obama quoted Rumi's line in one of his speeches: *"Out beyond ideas of wrongdoing and right doing, there is a field. I'll meet you there."* This message of finding common ground and moving beyond differences has resonated with many people, both within and outside politics.

5: Philosophers and Scientists

While it is impossible to establish a direct influence of Rumi's poetry on Einstein's theories, the striking similarities in their ideas are remarkable. Rumi's contemplations on time and space echo the themes Einstein explored through his thought experiments and scientific inquiries.

Rumi employs rich metaphors, symbols, and imagery to convey his understanding of space. He uses poetic language to evoke a sense of expansiveness and interconnectedness that transcends our limited perception. Rumi's symbolic language encourages us to embrace a more profound and inclusive understanding of space.

In his poem "*I am not this hair, I am not this skin,*" Rumi emphasizes that our true essence resides beyond the physical realm. By dissociating himself from physical attributes, Rumi points to a reality that extends beyond the confines of space as traditionally understood. This perspective resonates with Einstein's assertion that matter is not fundamental but a manifestation of energy, challenging our conventional understanding of space and physical existence.

Rumi and Einstein sought to understand the fundamental nature of reality and existence. Rumi's poetic insights often touch upon the timeless and interconnected aspects of the universe. At the same time, Einstein's theories of relativity revolutionized our understanding of space, time, and the fabric of the cosmos.

Rumi's Poetic Reflections on Time:

Rumi's poetry often contemplates the nature of time, transcending the conventional linear understanding. His verses suggest that time is not merely a linear progression but a multidimensional and fluid concept. Through his profound insights, Rumi encourages us to consider time as a transformative force that shapes our experiences and perceptions.

One of Rumi's poignant poems, "*The Drum of the Sky,*" evokes the idea of interconnectedness in relation to time. He speaks of the sky's drum, symbolizing the rhythmic pulsations of the universe, announcing the eternal union of the earth and the sky. Here, Rumi invites us to contemplate the timeless dance of existence, where past, present, and future converge.

"In the boundless realms where spirits soar,

Where stars like ancient drums roar,

A symphony of heavens plays on high,

The cosmic pulse, the drum of the sky.

With each celestial beat, worlds collide,

Galaxies dance, entwined in the cosmic tide,

Eternal rhythms, they serenade,

In the vast expanse, their echoes pervade.

Behold the moon, a luminescent guide,

Reflecting the drum's rhythm with pride,

The sun and planets join the celestial ballet,

Dancing to the drumbeat, night and day.

In the tapestry of space and time,

The drum's vibrations form a rhyme,

Each soul, a note in the grand design,

Playing our part within the divine.

O, seeker, listen to the celestial sound,

Beyond the stars, the drum is found,

Feel the rhythm in your heart's embrace,

And let your soul dance in cosmic grace.

When earthly worries weigh you down,

Look up, where heaven's drum is found,

Its melody reminds you, deep inside,

That life's a wondrous dance, open wide.

Embrace the beat, let your spirit fly,

As you dance with the drum of the sky,

In the harmony of the universe, you'll find,

Eternal bliss, with no end or bind."

Rumi's Contemplation of Space:

Rumi's poetic expressions also delve into space, challenging our conventional understanding of physical boundaries. His verses allude to the notion that space is not a separate entity but an interconnected fabric that unites all things.

In "*Love is the Force behind the Wheel of the Universe,*" Rumi encapsulates that love transcends spatial limitations. He suggests that love is a unifying force, enabling a harmonious interplay between beings and the cosmos. Rumi's perspective resonates with Einstein's theory of general relativity, which posits the interconnectedness of all matter and energy, shaping the fabric of space itself.

Rumi and Einstein, though separated by time and discipline, exemplify the human pursuit of truth in their diverse manifestations. By recognizing the parallels between mystical faith and scientific inquiry, we can transcend artificial boundaries and embrace a more comprehensive understanding of reality. Rumi's mystical faith and Einstein's scientific discoveries converge in their shared quest for truth, reminding us that different paths can lead to the same destination. By exploring their worldviews, we are invited to embark on a journey that transcends conventional divisions, fostering a harmonious relationship between mystical faith and scientific inquiry in our quest for a deeper understanding of the universe and ourselves.

"Lamps are different,

but the source of light is the same.

One matter, one energy, one into other."

In the above poem, it seems Rumi was aware of the relationship between matter and energy, which Einstein described in his famous formula. One could say that the idea for Einstein's theory already existed in a simple Rumi mystic poem. The more we know about the mystical philosophy of Rumi, the more questions come to mind about Rumi's understanding of the ultimate reality. As though Rumi had advanced knowledge of a different reality at the subatomic level, as in this poem, Rumi refers to a reality that is not physical.

"I am not this hair,

I am not this skin,

I am the spirit that lives within."

These questions come to mind once we learn more about the similarity between Rumi's philosophy of existence and the subatomic world.

Did Rumi know about the quantum field in the thirteenth century?

Did Rumi refer to the quantum field when discussing the spirit and heart's intuitive wisdom?

Did Rumi have extraordinary heart-intuitive wisdom about the ultimate reality that science was unaware of for more than seven hundred years?

While these questions could entertain us, a striking similarity exists between the metaphor and similes Rumi used to express his mystical view and the quantum field theory in the subatomic world! The field is the only reality that exists; everything is an illusion made up by our minds from the events that happened or did not happen in our Lives.

In conclusion, the influence of Rumi's poetry has been far-reaching, touching the lives of artists, writers, religious leaders, politicians, and thinkers worldwide. His message of universal love, spiritual connection, and emotional healing continues to inspire and uplift people today, and his legacy as a master poet and spiritual guide will undoubtedly continue to endure for generations to come.

Hegel, Rucker, and the Interpretation of Rumi's Pantheistic View

Rumi had a profound influence on Western intellectuals for centuries. Many philosophers and poets made Rumi famous in the West. It started with Joseph von Hammer-Purgstall, who, in 1889, translated and published some of Rumi's poetry. His translation was the first time the West got to know Rumi and became familiar with Masnavi, Rumi's epic book.

Purgstall's fascination with Rumi was unending. He wrote, "Rumi transcends not only the sun and the moon but also time and space, creation, and Judgment Day and reaches infinity. And from there, he attains the Absolute Being that is Everlasting and Ever present and represents the infinite love and lover."

Rückert, on the other hand, was the first to introduce the ghazal form of Rumi in German poetry. In 1819, he wrote, Ghaselen. This book was a collection of Rumi poems that reflected some of his work. In this book, Ruckert used Purgstall's translation. This book introduced Hegel, a German philosopher, to Rumi's poetry. In this book, Rucker used love, separation, unity, and longing to return to the source, Rumi's symbol that appeared in most of his work.

Hegel, a pantheist, fell in love with Rumi's poetry and believed that his teaching was a form of Pantheism, a belief that the universe is God. Hegel popularized the idea that Rumi was a proponent of Pantheism. Some believed that Hegel concluded that Rumi was a pantheist when he read this poem.

"Consciousness sleeps in minerals,
Dream in plants wakes up in animals,
Become self-aware in human."

In Pantheism, the follower believes that the universe is God, a clear distinction from Sufi's belief that Cosmo is a manifestation of God and divine energy. Hegel was unaware of Sufiism, and most of his knowledge about Rumi came from nineteen pages of Rucker's book.

Rumi's poetry is about the divine's love and returns to the source. Rumi believed in separation and then reunion. In contrast, In Pantheism, the idea of separation and returning to the source does not exist. This distinction is the most profound difference between mystic Sufi and Pantheism. However, there are some similarities between mystic Sufiism and Pantheism, written in Masnavi, but those ideas disappear once we understand separation and rejoining the source through the religion of love.

Hegel formed his idea on Rumi's pantheistic view by reading a part of Masnavi in Rucker's book and was unaware of symbolism and metaphors in Rumi's poetry, which is the basis for all his poetry.

Sufi philosopher Ibn Arabi said, "Nothing real exists besides God, who discloses himself In and through the universe."

Rumi held this belief that God reveals Himself in the universe, which is the manifestation of God, not that the universe is the God as in Pantheism. This concept of God is a clear distinction between Sufiism and Pantheism. Once we understand these profound differences, we can conclude that Sufism is not Pantheism and Rumi was not a pantheist.

In Pantheism, God is not distinct from the universe; in Sufiism, God is separate from the universe and manifests himself in the universe, which is the energy behind the creation of Cosmo.

Many pantheists hold two separate views of God and the universe. For example, Aquinas distinguishes God as the form and matter of all things. These varying beliefs in Pantheism could also be the reason behind Hegel's view of Rumi.

In many cases, this differentiation between Pantheism and Sufiism is not well drawn and leads many to believe that Sufism is a form of Pantheism. Rumi believed that the entire universe is created from one source. He said that the source of consciousness runs through everything in the universe. Rumi quoted this verse from the Quran as a religious scholar in many of his writings.

"The God proportioned you and breathed something of its spirit into your soul." Quran 32:9

Rumi's belief in universal consciousness and man's divinity within is the inspiration for his poetry. We can't have a meaningful understanding of Rumi's poetry if we do not understand Rumi's Philosophy of universal consciousness as a source and everything in the universe as a part of that source.

Masnavi, A Mystical Masterpiece

Rumi, a 13th-century Persian poet, theologian, and mystic, is significant in spiritual literature and inspires readers worldwide. His teachings revolve around returning to the source through the religion of Love. According to Rumi, love is not merely an emotion or a romantic concept but a transformative force that can lead us back to our true essence.

"Kindle the candle in your heart.

Fill the void in your spirit.

The yearning to return to the source,

Planted in each of us by the source."

One of Rumi's most significant contributions to spiritual literature is his magnum opus, The Masnavi. This epic mystic poetry holds immense importance in the realm of Rumi's teachings, encapsulating his wisdom and serving as a guiding light for seekers of truth and divine connection.

Masnavi is a book of mystic poetry written in Persian. It comprises six books, each with stories and anecdotes in verse — the book has 25,000 verses or 50,000 lines. Each story has a meaning of love, compassion, and humanity. The core message of the *Masnavi* is the unification with the beloved through the *Mazehab Ishq.*

Masnavi begins with a powerful and evocative poem called The Poem of Reed. This introductory piece sets the tone for the entire work, conveying a heartfelt lamentation of separation and longing. This poem's reed represents the human soul, symbolizing the innate yearning to return to its source. It cries out, expressing the pain of being severed from its origin, and seeks reunion with the beloved.

Rumi's choice to start The Masnavi with the poem of Reed is deliberate and significant.

"Listen to the sound of the Reed as it tells a tale,

Complaining and crying about separation

Saying, ever since I was cut from the Reedbed,

I made this crying sound.

Anyone apart from someone he loves

Understand what I say.

Anyone pulled away from a source,

Longing to go back to its source."

It serves as a prelude to the teachings that unfold throughout the rest of the work. The poem encapsulates the fundamental theme of returning to the source through the religion of Love, laying the groundwork for the transformative journey Rumi invites his readers to embark upon.

The creation of the *Masnavi* was a labor of love that spanned over twenty years of Rumi's life. It was not a work produced hastily or without deep contemplation. Rumi's journey in crafting the

Masnavi involved a profound exploration of mystical experiences, philosophical insights, and divine inspiration. He drew from his spiritual awakening and encounters with his beloved spiritual guide, Shams Tabrizi.

Throughout these twenty years, Rumi refined his poetic voice and honed his teachings, infusing them into the tapestry of *The Masnavi*. The work evolved organically, with Rumi weaving together various stories, parables, and verses to convey profound spiritual truths. *The Masnavi* became a vessel for Rumi's wisdom, providing readers with a roadmap to navigate the complexities of human existence and find unity with the beloved.

Rumi's dedication to the *Masnavi* shows his commitment to guiding others toward spiritual enlightenment. It is a testament to his belief in the transformative power of poetry and the written word. *The Masnavi* stands as a testament to Rumi's profound spiritual insights and ability to convey complex philosophical concepts in a way that resonates with readers across cultures and generations.

Within the pages of the *Masnavi*, readers are invited to embark on a transformative journey of self-discovery and divine connection. Rumi's teachings, nurtured and distilled over two decades, offer guidance, solace, and inspiration. Through the diverse stories, parables, and mystical narratives within the *Masnavi*, Rumi's timeless wisdom illuminates the path toward unity with the beloved, guiding seekers to reconnect with their true selves and the divine source.

Rumi's poetry covers diverse philosophical and mystic topics, expressing his love for his beloved and his yearning to return to him.

In *Masnavi's* second book, his poetry covered many topics filled with anecdotes, life lessons, moral stories, personal growth, and stories from all religions. Rumi doesn't offend anyone and includes everyone. Rumi's poetry is about hearts, emotions, feelings, and instincts. After meeting his mentor, Shams, he moved from a purely intellectual scholar to a mystic poet.

To enjoy Rumi's poetry, one must read *Masnavi* and understand the symbols and metaphors Rumi used to convey his thoughts and beliefs on the divinity within, the destruction of self, reunion with the beloved, and the heart's intuitive wisdom. Rumi wrote *Masnavi* in the poetic form called couplets, which means *Masnavi*. *Masnavi* is full of Divine love. *Mazehab Ishq* (Religious of love) was the only religious Rumi followed.

Most of the stories and poems in *Masnavi* are Symbolism and teach Rumi's Philosophy of life, spirituality, and the road of love to join the beloved. There is a beneath-the-surface meaning to Rumi's poems and stories that have captured people's imaginations worldwide for centuries.

Though rooted in his religion and culture, Rumi's mystic poetry carries the central message of love through allegories, analogies, symbols, and metaphors. Rumi's message of love is to raise humanity above the narrow confines of race, gender, class, religion, tribe, and nation.

At the heart of Rumi's *Masnavi* is a fundamental message of compassion, peace, and justice.
In this part of this book, we study a few tales of Rumi in *Masnavi* and discuss the metaphor and symbolism, which is the core of Rumi's poetry.

The beauty of Rumi's poetry and his use of symbols and metaphors to express his thought is not bound to one interpretation. We may have a different take on the same story or poems in *Masnavi* based on our core beliefs, ideas, thoughts, and upbringing, the way Rumi intended everyone to enjoy his poetry and interpret it based on their understanding.

There is no right or wrong way to explain Rumi's poetry and tales in *Masnavi* if we know the core beliefs of Rumi: the divinity within, love, reunification with the beloved, destruction of the Illusionary self (ego), and intuitive heart wisdom.

In the West, Rumi's primary recognition stems from the work of Coleman Barks, who does not read or write Farsi and is not a scholar of Islam. He is a poet and an enthusiast of Rumi's poetry.

Coleman is completely upfront that he doesn't translate Rumi's poems from the original Farsi. He said, "My theory is that you cannot be a poet in a language you didn't hear in a cradle."

Coleman describes Rumi's poetry as "the mystery of opening the heart; you can't say it in a language."

The King and the enslaved girl is the first story in *Masnavi*. In this story, Rumi illustrates that we cannot reach our beloved if we live in a world of illusionary self. We need to destroy our illusionary self (*Fana*) to reach our true self (*Bagha)*

The King and the Slave Girl

A Powerful king left his palace, riding on his Arabian horse for a hunting trip, followed by his *Wazir*, minister, guardsmen, and hunting dogs. As he was passing through the Bazaar of a small village, his eyes fell on a slave girl who was standing by the side of a shop. The king's heartbeat became faster, and the blood rushed to his face. The king asked his *Wazir* about the girl that captured his eyes.

His *Wazir* becomes aware that the king's breathing is faster and realizes he cannot reign over his horse. Sensing the king's condition, The *Wazir* got off his horse, approached the king, and said, "My king, are you okay?"

The king took a deep breath and said, "Return to the palace."

"Is something wrong, my king? Should I send for a *Hakim*?"

"No, I feel awkward; need to return to Palace."

The *Wazir* ordered the guardsman to return to the palace. On the way back, the *Wazir* rode by the king's side.

The king got off his horse, entered the palace, and summoned his *Wazir* into his chamber. The *Wazir* stood before the king with his hands crossed on his abdomen. The king sipped the water and said, "Who was that girl?"

With a bowed head, the *Wazir* said, "My king, she is a slave, and his master brought her to the bazaar to sell."

The king wrinkled his forehead and said, "Get gold from the treasury and bring that girl to the palace."

"Yes, my King."

The *Wazir* mounted his horse and rode to the Bazaar and saw the girl was still standing at the same place where the king saw her. He paid the owner and helped the girl to ride on another horse between him and a guardsman.

After he arrived, *Wazir* notified the king that the slave girl was in the palace. The king ordered his *Wazir* to take the girl into the *Haram* and ask everyone to leave her room. He walked the long pathway to the *Haram*. The woman in charge of the *Haram* affair directed the king to the slaved girl's room.

He talked with the girl for a long time and left her room. He asked the woman in charge of the *Haram* to take the girl to the *Hamam* for a full bath and purchase her the most expensive silk dress in the Bazaar. Before leaving the *Haram*, he said, "Make sure you pay as much attention to her as you do to the queen."

The *Haram* manager bowed and said, "Yes, my king."

A few days later, the girl fell sick and became pale and weak. Upon learning about the girl's sickness, the king asked his *Wazir* to bring the finest *Hakims*, even if it was in another country. The *Wazir* summoned the well-known *Hakims* from his own country and Samarkand, the neighboring country. But none of the *Hakim* could cure her disease. Her condition worsened, and she stopped eating and drinking.

The king asked his *Wazir* to prepare the mosque, as he wanted to spend the night inside the mosque. The *Wazir* was surprised by the king's unexpected request and followed his order. The king prayed and cried his eyes out inside the mosque. By midnight he was so exhausted that he fell asleep. He dreamed that a charismatic spiritual Wiseman would tell him, "Tomorrow, a spiritual *Hakim* will come to your palace, and he is the only man to cure the slave girl. Listen to him and follow all his suggestions if you want the girl to live."

In the morning, the king woke up with renewed happiness and asked his *Wazir* to notify him when the spiritual *Hakim* showed up.

Wazir followed the order but was worried that the king was losing his mind. That night, the king did not get much sleep. In the morning, the king and his *Wazir* walked to the gate of the Palace, and after a few minutes, an image appeared behind the big oak tree. The king said, "he is coming."

Wazir's eyes wandered around, but he saw no one walking toward the Palace gate. *Wazir* took a deep breath, rubbed his forehead, and said, "My King, I do not see anyone."

The king said, "Look closer behind the tree."

Wazir cupped his hand on his forehead and saw an older man with a cane walking toward them. The man was in a completely white garment. After arriving at the gate, the king accompanied the spiritual *Hakim* to the *Haram*.

There, *Hakim* sat on the ground and asked everyone to leave the room, including the King. The king waited in the next room. The *Hakim* took his bag off his neck and put it beside him. He asked the girl a few questions while holding her hand to check her pulse.

The girl was so frail that *Hakim* had to wait a few seconds to hear her respond. The Hakim dampened the cloth, rubbed it around her lips, and encouraged her to sip water. The Hakim waited, and after a few minutes, the girl answered his question. There was no change in her pulse or facial expression throughout the questioning.

When he asked, "Where did you live before?"

Hakim noticed that her pulse rate had changed. Then he asked about the village and the street where she lived. As *Hakim* asked about her house on that street, her pulse increased, and the blood flashed to her pale face.

The girls started sharing more information with *Hakim*. She told him about a man she fell in love with. Then *Hakim* asked the girl, "What was his job."

"Goldsmith"

Hakim noticed that life rushed into her body; a blush of red ran down her face, and she became as lovely as a red rose.

Hakim left the room and told the King he knew what was wrong with the girl. The King was happy, and the smile returned to his face. The king asked, "What was wrong with her?'
"I need to tell you in private," *Hakim* said. *Hakim* and the king walked to the main palace.

Hakim asked the king if he wanted to be alone with him. The King signaled his *Wazir* to leave the room.

The king faced *Hakim*, put his arms on his lap, and said, "Did you give her the herbs?"

The *Hakim* ran his hand through his thick white beard and said, "My lord, the herbs can't cure her."

The king leaned back on his thorn, squinted, wrinkled his forehead, and said, "You told me you could cure her."

"Yes, I can cure her, but not with herbs."

"Then, what is her sickness that you cannot cure with herbs."

"Love"

The *Hakim* tells the king that the slave girl is in love with a Goldsmith from Samarkand, and the only way that the girl can survive is to unite her with the Goldsmith.

The king remembered his dream, "follow all the suggestions from the spiritual man if you want the slave girl to live."

The King sent his *Wazir* to bring the goldsmith from Samarkand. After the slave girl and the goldsmith reunited, the girl became happy and healthy again.

After six months, the spiritual *Hakim* returned to check on the slave girl. He prepared a potion and gave it to the goldsmith to drink. The next day the goldsmith fell ill. He got weaker and paler daily; his face wrinkled, and his cheek sank. He lost weight and was not that handsome stud man like before.

The slave girl slowly lost interest in him. She now felt more for the king than for the goldsmith. After the goldsmith died, the slave girl was in love with the king and thought she had found her true love."

Moral of the story:

Rumi used symbolism and metaphor in this story to describe the illusionary self or ego, source or true self. This story is like a play, with different players playing different roles.

The king is the true self, the Hakim is the spiritual leader, and the goldsmith is the ego or illusionary self. The girl is the part that is attached to ego, beauty, and wealth. For the slave girl to connect with the source or her true self, the illusionary self, the goldsmith, must be killed.

Rumi says to join the source through the religion of love and attain infinite wisdom and happiness, we must kill the *Nafs* or illusionary self.

The Parrot and the Merchant:

A merchant brought a sweet-talking parrot from India. He learned so many new and funny words that mesmerized anyone who came to listen to him. Soon he became the favorite bird among the townspeople.

People enjoyed being in his company, and he entertained everyone who came to see the family.

The merchant planned another trip to India to sell more merchandise at the bazaar.

As customary, he asked his wife, children, and close friends what they wanted to receive as a gift.

He was about to leave when he said, "I didn't say goodbye to my best friend and didn't ask him what he wanted me to bring him from India."

He stood before the cage, patted the Parrot with his finger, and asked, "I am going back to your birthplace. What do you want me to bring for you?"

The Parrot paused briefly and said, "I don't ask for any gift, but I ask you for a favor."

"What is that you have in mind?"

The parrot said, "I want you to see my family and friends and let them know I live with you. They are worried about me. They even don't know if I am still alive."

"Where can I find them?" the merchant asked.

The Parrot said, "As you enter India, the first village is my place. I lived there all my life before you brought me to Persia."

The merchant tightened his bags on his horse and started his journey to India, wondering why his Parrot wanted him to visit his place.

After a few days of arduous traveling, he arrived in India and searched for his parrot homestead. He asked many people on his way about where all the parrots in this city live. They gave him the direction, and he reached a lush garden after a day of walking and riding on his horse.

As he entered the garden, he was surrounded by green hills, running rivers, and colorful flowers everywhere. He sat by the river, splashed water on his face, and drank water when the birds singing echoed in the garden. He followed the direction of the sound and arrived at the green field.

He asked where all the other parrots were. The guard's Parrot said, "They are napping on the tree branches."

"Can you ask your folks to gather here? I have a message for you from one of your friends."

The bird made a piercing sound. All the Parrots flew and surrounded the merchant.

The merchant took a moment to admire the beauty that surrounded him. He has seen nothing like this before. He felt happy and at peace and forgot about all his troubles for a moment.

One Parrot said, "We are here to listen to what message you brought from our friend?"

The merchant said, "Your friend is happy and healthy. He lives in my house, and we all love him."

One parrot flew and perched on a tree branch as he finished his words. He fluttered, fell, and died. The merchant was saddened by what he said and wished he had never come and brought the message.

He left the garden with a feeling of sadness in his heart. In the next few days, he purchased all the merchandise he needed for his trade and all the gifts for his family and friends and started the journey back home. After a month of traveling, he arrived home. The next day friends gathered in his home to welcome his arrival. He opened his luggage and gave everyone their gifts.

Then he stood before the cage and said, "My dear Parrot, I found your place and gave your message to your friend. I think you had a very close friend there. He fell from the tree and died when I told them you live with me. I am very sorry."

Once the merchant finished talking, his Parrot fluttered, hitting himself on the cage a few times before crashing onto the floor.

The merchant cried inconsolably, "What is in my messages that kill parrots?"

After he regained his composure, he opened the cage, gently removed his parrot, and put him on the ground. While he was closing the cage door, the Parrot flew and perched on the tree in the courtyard.

The merchant was amazed and shocked, "was this a trick to leave the cage? Where did you learn it?"

The Parrot said, "You brought me the message about escaping prison!"

"How?"

"When my brother parrot fell on the ground, he pretended to be dead to send a message to me on how to escape from my prison."

With a puzzled eye, the merchant asked, "What was on that message?"

"My brother said that my sweet voice and beauty are the reason for my imprisonment. And he showed me how to escape."

The Parrot finished his talk, said goodbye to his old family, and flew to a place where he belonged. He longed to return to his original home and be in his family's company.

Moral of the story:

Here again, Rumi uses metaphor to explain that we are separated from our source, longing to return. Our attachments to material, wealth, and beauty prevent us from returning.

Our illusionary self prevents us from returning to our original place. Once we kill that ego, we have the key to escape and return to our home, where we can find true happiness; This is our true self, a part of universal consciousness longing to return to the source. The killing of the bird is a metaphor for killing the ego. Once the ego is destroyed, the true self is to join the source, "spirit, universal consciousness or God."

The Poor Man and the Diamond

A poor man in the city was tired of being unable to support his family. One night he prayed and asked God to help him to provide food for his family, and he could not take it anymore.

In his dream, he was told to go to a bookshop in the main bazaar. Find the wrinkled paper in that bookstore and follow the directions. In the morning, he went to the bookshop. He looked everywhere and couldn't find the letter. He investigated the trash and found the letter he saw in his dream. He picked up the letter and read it when he left the bookshop.

The letter stated that there was a shrine close to the palace. Under the pomegranate tree, you find a bow and arrow. Stand under the tree with your back behind the shrine. Put the arrow in the bow, and where the arrow points, you will find a precious diamond so unique that only one exists in the entire world.

The poor man followed the direction and dug where the arrow fell. He repeated the process for many days but didn't find any diamonds. Tired and frustrated, he prayed to God to solve this mystery and direct him to the location of the diamond. His prayer was answered.

One day he heard the voice, "I told you to put the arrow in the bow and don't throw. When you pulled the bow, why didn't you look at the back of the arrow instead of the head? The back of the arrow pointed directly at the diamond. You searched outside you; the arrow was pointing inside you."

Moral of the story:

We search outside for wealth, fame, and money without realizing that the source of everything we want is inside us. We need to tap into this eminence wisdom to get what we want. We can't find what we're looking for outside ourselves. We are that unique diamond. There is no one like us if we know where to look.

"The cave you fear to enter,

May hide the light you seek."

"You wander from one village to another, searching for the diamond necklace already around your neck!"

The Greek and the Chinese Painter

There was a rivalry between Chinese and Greek painters for a long time. This rivalry had been going on for so long that the king decided to intervene and settle this matter.

He asked his head minister to create a competition between these two painters so that he could decide who was the best.

The minister created the contests by presenting the painters with two old and rundown cottages on the hunting field that once were the king's hunting cabins.

He asked the painters to show their skills by painting the old cottages. Mildew, dust, and tree branches covered the cottage's walls, barely visible from a distance. The minister took the painters to the cottage and ordered the palace manager to provide the painters with whatever they requested with no money spared.

The Chinese Painter asked for various brushes and colors, and the Greek Painter asked for nothing.

They both moved to their assigned cottage and started working on the project of their lifetime.

The Chinese Painter cut all the tree branches and removed overgrown, dead bushes surrounding the cottage. He then applied base paint on the cabin. After a few days of grueling cutting and eliminating the debris, he started painting. He drew a template and divided the cottage wall into distinct sections. After he finished his sketches, he started his delicate painting. First, he used large brushes and then razor-thin to create the details of his artwork. He made such a masterpiece that the wall looked like a bouquet of colorful flowers.

The Greek Painter was also busy for a few days cutting the tree branches and making sure nothing obscured the reflection of the house falling on the river by the cottage. After finishing his arduous work, he removed all the mildew collected after years of neglect. He scrubbed and polished the old paint and dust after removing all the mold from the cottage's surface. He turned the cottage into a mirror to reflect without any obstruction.

While the Chinese Painter was busy creating a palace of the dream, the Greek Painter was scrubbing and polishing the old cottage.

After days of hard work, judgment day was approaching fast. The palace invited all artists to accompany the king to select the winner of the best painter competition.

The minister notified the king that the painters had finished their work. On the day of the competition, the king and his entourage walked toward the cottages to view the work of the best painters. After he got closer to the cabins, the workers removed an enormous curtain, and a palace of colors and design appeared that froze the king on his path. He stopped from a distance and admired the work and artistry of the Chinese Painter. He was transfixed by the beauty of the cottage, which was turned into a piece of art. The king couldn't take his eyes off the Chinese cottage. But it was time to view the cottage that showcased the creek artwork.

As he got closer to the Greek cottage, he saw that everything from the old cabin had been removed. It has been polished and refined to the degree that it reflects all the beauty surrounding the cottage; the tree, flowers, clouds, and even the beauty of the Chinese cottage are reflected on the wall of the Greek cabin.

The king thought that the beauty Greek Painter created was from the inside and could not be destroyed by environmental factors such as rain or wind, but the next rain could ruin the beauty that the Chinese painter created. So, this thinking made the king's decision easy, and he declared the Greek Painter the best Painter in the city.

Moral of the story:

Rumi compares the heart to a mirror. A mirror cannot reflect when it is covered with dust.

"The beauty you see in me is a reflection of you."

He compares ego, jealousy, and hate to the dust in the mirror. Our hearts can't reflect all the beauty and love when filled with ego, jealousy, and hate. We must remove the dust from the mirror to reflect and see the love and true beauty.

He compares the Chinese painting to the beauty and wealth, which we can lose in the blink of the eyes like rain washing all the paint from the Chinese painting. Our beauty is washed away as we get older. Our wealth can be destroyed without any notice. But if we have a clean and polished heart, nothing can ruin it, even a downpour.

"Your task is not to seek love, but to find and remove all the barriers within yourself that you have built against it."

Here Rumi points to inner beauty. We need to remove the barrier (ego) for the heart to reflect all other beauties surrounding us, including the beauty of love. We don't need to create a masterpiece painting.

"The only infinite beauty is the beauty of the heart."

Humility

Ayaz was a confident and unique minister to Sultan Mahmood. He was so close to the king that he made other ministers and employees jealous of his position. He occupied a small room beside the servant quadrant to live in the palace. He did not bring much when he moved into the castle.

Ayaz had a habit of going a few times to his room during the day. This habit made other ministers suspicious, and they planned to tell the Sultan about Ayaz disappearing in his room at different times of the day.

Other ministers came up with dubious suspicions of the Ayaz's activity. Finally, a powerful minister told the king, "We should investigate Ayaz. He goes to his room multiple times a day. He might be stealing palace treasure and hiding it in his room. We must find out if he is loyal to you or misuses your trust."

The king was confident of Ayaz's loyalty and never doubted him. He asked his *Wazir* to keep order and discipline, "What should we do?"

Without hesitation, the *Wazir* said, "We should search his room."

The Sultan ordered the search, confident they wouldn't find anything that made him distrust Ayaz.

The *Wazir* accompanied his guard with the investigation. They looked everywhere in the room but couldn't find anything except a broken wooden box holding a few torn, old, dirty pieces of clothing and shoes.

The *Wazir* told his guards, "Ayaz is a clever minister; he might have buried the gold and treasures."

They dug everywhere inside and outside the room but found nothing.

The *Wazir* reluctantly told the Sultan that they found only a box with old, wrinkled clothes and torn shoes."

The Sultan knew that he had never distrusted his most loyal minister, but he wondered about the clothes and his visit to his room during work. He asked to meet Ayaz in private. Ayaz entered the place. The Sultan asked him to sit in a humongous gold-decorated chair before him. He said, "I ordered the search of your room, not because I lost my trust in you. I did it to stop the rumors, once and for all."

Ayaz said, "I know, my Sultan, that you never doubt my loyalty; it didn't bother me. "

The Sultan said, "But I was surprised at what was in your room. You are the palace's powerful minister; why keep old, torn clothes in your room? You can purchase the most expensive silk clothing at the bazaar.

"My Sultan. As You know, I was a poor man before you brought me to the palace. These are the memories of my poverty. I wear them each morning before the palace to remind myself of my true self. I don't want to forget who I am. These clothes remind me of my poverty and help me feel for your kingdom's poor and disadvantaged people. These memories give me the strength to help other people. It connects me with them."

Moral of the story:

We should never forget who we are and where we came from. Don't attach to the material world. Attachments make us lose our true identity. Attachment to the material is the reason for our ego. Lose your ego to find your true self.

The Lover who Was Nothing

A madly-in-love man arrived at the house of his beloved and knocked on the door.

"Who is it?" The woman asked.

"It is me." the man responded.

The woman said, "Go away. There is no place for a man like you in this home. You are not ready to become my lover. You still tell "me" while declaring your love to me. There is no distinction between lover and beloved. Come back when you are ready to be my lover."

The man, disappointed, walked away and traveled for some time, burning in the fire of separation. He spent time in a faraway land, met many people, and learned about love and longing to join his beloved. He came to the house of the woman again and knocked. The woman asked, "Who is it?"

"No one. The one on this side of the door is also you." The man said.

The woman said, "Now that you don't see yourself, you become me. There is only room for one person in this house."

She opened the door and welcomed her lover inside. "Now, there is no difference between you and me. We are one and of the same."

Moral of the story:

Liberation from the illusionary self.

"O beloved, take me from me,

And fill me with your love,

And free me from this world.

If my heart is on anything but you,

Let the fire burn me from the inside."

We must destroy the illusionary self and detach ourselves from the material world to join the beloved. True love does need any worldly things. In the world of divinity within, there is no duality, just one.

"If you do not find me from within

You would never find me.

I have been with You,

from the beginning."

"I searched for God and found myself.
I searched for myself and found God."

"Your soul and mine are the same.
We appear and disappear in each other."

Setting an Example

The Oghuz Turkmens were wild and fierce warriors. They invaded many cities in Persia, killing their inhabitants and stealing their goods and treasure.

One day, they arrived in a city and saw two older men sitting in front of their hut. One was the village headmaster, and the other one was his neighbor.

The Turkman soldier got off his horse and approached the older men.

The village headmaster said, "You are the great warrior. You invaded and conquered many cities in Persia. What do you get from killing an old, wasted man like me?"

The soldier said, "I kill you to set an example for your neighbor telling where he hid the gold."

The headmaster shook his head, "what gold? He is poorer than I am. He doesn't have any gold."

The soldier wrinkled his forehead, "an informant told us that he hid his treasure."

The headmaster said, "Why you don't kill him to set an example for me, and I will show you where I am hiding my gold?"

Moral of the story:

To find the gold, one needs to kill the Illusionary self. In this story, the headmaster's neighbor is the ego. Once the soldier kills the neighbor (ego), he can find the treasures (true self) buried inside by the illusionary self.

"Kill the cow of your ego so that your inner spirit (true self) can come to life and attain true awareness."

The King's Eagle

The king raised an eagle in the palace when he was little. He cared for the eagle and spent much time with him, loving him like his child.

One morning, he walked to the room where he kept the eagle and noticed he was not there. He summoned the palace guard and searched the entire palace. King himself took part in the search. They searched day and night but couldn't locate the eagle. The king stayed awake the whole night to welcome his bird back home. He was crushed when the guards returned without the eagle.

The next day, the king's army started the search; they went to every home in the city.

The eagle flew around the town and sat on the roof of an older woman. The woman brought the bird into his home. "You must have had a bad life in the hands of someone who did not take good care of you. Your owner must be an unkind person. He didn't cut your feathers and nails for a long time. I am glad that you escaped from that cruel life. I take good care of you."

The older woman sharpened her scissors and cut most of the eagle feathers and nails.

When the soldier entered her house, they recognized the bird without feathers and nails. They immediately notified the king. The king ordered them to wait until he came and brought his eagle to the palace.

When the king entered the house, the bird came to him. When he saw the bird, he started crying.

"Why did you leave your palace to come to this ruined house? Where are your beautiful nails and feathers? Now you can't fly or hunt. This is the punishment for your disloyalty. It is your punishment for leaving the people who truly know you and staying in the company of those who judge you by your appearance.

Moral of the story:

Happiness and the good life are about spending time with the people who know you for the person you are. They don't judge you. They accept you as you are, not as you appear.

The people that don't know you well can hurt you without knowing that their actions and words can hurt you.

"Be with those who help your being."

"Everything that is made beautiful is made for the eye of one who sees."

"Always search for your true nature in those you are with, as rose oil comes from roses."

The Night Guardsman and the Drunk

A night guardsman was patrolling the street when he came across a drunk man leaning against the wall. He approached the man, patted his shoulder, and said, "Hey, what are you doing this late at night sitting on the street?"

There is no response from the man. He shook his shoulder hard and yelled. "Are you drunk? Tell me what you have been drinking?"

The man opened his eyes and threw his hand in the air, pointing to an empty bottle across him. "I drank what was on that empty bottle."

The night guardsman picked up the bottle and sniffed inside the bottle. He said, "Did you drink wine? You know drinking wine is illegal. Tell me again if you have drunk the wine."

With a slurred speech, the man said, "You are the wise man; you should know."

The night guardsman was frustrated and decided to try another approach to determine if this man was drunk.

He yelled at the drunk man. "Open your mouth and say, ah."

The drunk man reluctantly opened his mouth and said, "Hu."

The guardsman snapped. "I told you to say ah, not Hu."

The drunk man said, "I'm ecstatic. The ah is for unhappy people like you, wasting their time. I'm always happy, and the sound of Hu comes from people who are happy where they are in their life."

The night guardsman grabbed the drunk man and yelled. "Get up. I'll take you in now. I'm done with your rhetoric and false spirituality."

The drunk man pulled his hand away. "If I reason like a wise and clever man, I will sit in my shop and make money."

The drunk man leaned back on the wall and closed his eyes, instantly falling asleep, snoring.

The night guard man, exasperated, walked off and left him alone.

Moral of the story:

Find yourself in your heart, not in your Mind.

"Sale your cleverness and buy bewilderment."

"I am drunk, and you are insane,

Who's going to take us home."

"I'm in such shape today,

That I don't know which is the thorn,

And which is the rose,

My love put me in this shape today,

I don't know who the lover is,

And who is the beloved?

Yesterday's drunkenness led me,

To the door of my love,

But today I can't find the door

Or The house."

Juhi at the Funeral

A young Juhi was accompanying his father to the funeral of a relative. He listened to the son of the deceased walking behind the dead coffin and crying out his delirious grief.

"My beloved father, where are they taking you? Are they burying your body in a dark place with no door, window, or light? Do they leave you in a place where the sun never shines? You were a man of respect; how could you accept to make this your permanent house? You could have chosen the best home in the city."

When the young Juhi heard the son's words, he faced his dad and said, "Father, do they take the body to our house?'

His father wrinkled his forehead and squinted. "don't be an idiot. What a stupid question! "

"But father, all the detail the young man described point to our house. Listen to him carefully, and you will understand what I mean. You don't see and hear it. Our house is missing everything that boy said: no door, roof, or window. The sun never shines in our house."

Moral of the story:

A house without love is like a house without a window and door. The sun never shines there.

"I said to the night,

If you are in love with the moon,

It is because you never stay for long.

The night turned to me and said,

It is not my fault. I never see the Sun,

how can I know that love is endless?"

The Tree of Eternal Life

A rumor spread in an Arabian town about a tree in India whose fruit bestowed eternal life.

The king became aware of this fantastic tree in India. He summoned his most trusted minister and told him about the tree. He asked his minister to travel to India and take as many funds as needed for his trip. He also provided him with the best horse in his kingdom.

The minister got everything he needed for this long and challenging journey. After months of travel, he arrived in India and started asking people about this tree: its fruit gives eternal life to anyone who eats it. He traveled from city to city, passing mountains, forests, and deserts, asking everyone on his way.

Most people he asked about the tree ignored him, and some laughed at him. Others teased him, giving him a direction that didn't exist. A year passed, but he couldn't find the tree.

He loved the king very much and didn't want to disappoint him. Despite not having much hope of finding such a tree, he continued his journey for many months.

He finally concluded that his search for the eternal tree was just an illusion and would never find such a tree. His hope dwindled, and he decided to return to his country.

On his way back, he decided to visit a famous Sufi and get his blessing. After a long search, he found this spiritual Sufi living in a remote mountain cave. He spent the night in a caravansary in the city, and the following day he started his journey to meet this wise man.

After two days of walking, he finally met his hero. Once he looked into his eyes, he started crying uncontrollably. The spiritual man patted his back and asked him to come inside. After he composed himself, he told the Sufi about his journey to find this eternal tree.

The Sufi said, "This eternal tree is the knowledge in your heart. It is the wisdom of the heart. It has many names, trees, seas, and clouds. This knowledge in your heart is accessible once you remove the ego. You become your true self. Your true self never dies. There is no duality."

The minister ran his hand through his thick grey beard and said, "How can I connect with this heart knowledge?"

The Sufi said, "You access this true knowledge of your heart by destroying the illusionary self. Once you access the heart's knowledge, the illusionary self disappears, and your true self never dies. It happens that you get to know this heart knowledge as a tree. Go to your city; the tree is already inside you."

The Sufi thanked the wise man and kissed his hand. Before he said goodbye to his master, the Sufi gave him a loaf of bread for his long journey.

The minister's immense burden was lifted from his shoulder, and he no longer felt defeated. His heart opened, and he knew his journey home would be much easier.

Moral of the story:

Finding the eternal tree is accessing the heart's intelligence. Destruction of the illusionary self gives you access to the heart's intelligence where duality doesn't exist. You join the source and become one.

"You travel from village to village on your horse, asking everyone, has anyone seen my horse?"

"Don't look for the remedy for your troubles outside yourself. You are the medicine. You are the cure for your sorrow.

"Don't go on a journey to find eternal life. The great journey starts from where you are. You are the world. You have everything you need."

All Roads End at one Destination.

Four men traveled in the same caravan all day but had not spoken with each other. Most travelers went to *Caravanserai* to eat and sleep when the caravan stopped for the night. But these four men were laborers without money to eat or sleep inside the *Caravanserai*.

They made a fire outside and gathered around the fire. All four men were from four different countries and spoke other languages. The younger man was from Persia, the older man was an Arab, the third one was Turkish, and the fourth man was from Greek. The weather was freezing, and the four men were tired, cold, and hungry.

A kind fellow traveler saw the men and walked outside. He paid them some money to buy food for dinner.

As the traveler left, the Persian said, "We should buy grapes. It is cheap here."

The Greek man said, "I don't want whatever the Persian man wants. I want to buy grapes."

The Turkish guy said, "I don't want whatever you two guys want. I like grapes."

The Arab said, "I don't care what you guys want; I want grapes for dinner."

The argument continued without knowing that they all wanted the same thing. A fight broke out, and the men started hitting each other when a wise man heard the commotion and ran toward them. He managed to stop the war. He spoke all four languages.

They soon learned they all wanted the same thing, and all this fighting was for nothing.

Moral of the story:

Throughout history, wars and conflicts resulted from race, nation, and religion. Rumi was in the middle of this conflict when moguls invaded Afghanistan, and he had to leave his country and migrate to Konya, today's Turkey.

All religions walk different paths to reach one God. They all want the same thing, a union with the beloved. But they don't know that their destinations are all the same.

Our differences are in our ignorance of each other.

> *"All religions are singing the same song."*
> *The sun's light looks different*
> *on this wall than it does on that wall,*
> *but it's still the same light."*

The Desire to Return to the Source

A storm pushed a cluster of duck eggs from the coast to the ocean. Their mother created a haven for them under trees lined up along the shore. As they were floating on the foaming wave, the tide pushed one of the eggs away and separated it from the other. The force of the wave hit the egg onto a rock, and the shell broke. A tiny duckling poked its head from the cracked shell, trying to free itself from the shell.

The exhausted little duckling is trying to get to the shore but struggling against the force of the wave. Another strong wave pushed the duck close to the coast, and he managed to walk on the dry land for the first time. The duck was walking along the shore, unable to keep its balance, falling on the ground repeatedly.

A hen walking along the vast shore saw the duck struggling to walk and keep itself uptight. The hen eggs had just hatched, and she had to care for her babies. But she stopped by and brought the tired and hungry duck under her wing with much kindness.

The babies grew up together and could feed themselves without their mothers' help.

The duck had an intense urge to go to the water all the time, but he was afraid of the ocean and did not want to lose the comfort of what he already had. He couldn't comprehend the intense feeling of returning to the sea to his siblings as they never desired to go to the water. There were days that he wanted the safety of the shore, but there were also days that he longed to go back to where he came from. He was unable to make his final decision. He also knew that staying in the safety of the shore could be a prison without a wall for him.

Moral of the story:

The purpose of our life is to return to the source. The impulse and desire to join the source are within us. Longing to return to the source through the religion of love is the inspiration for Rumi's mystical poetry. Our attachment to the illusionary self prevents us from making the final decision and joining the source where we can find true happiness and the super divine power inside us.

In this story, the duckling intensely desires to return to its source, water. But the illusionary self prevents the duckling from returning to the water. The illusionary self thinks about the shore's safety and the fear of returning to the ocean. This fear of the unknown keeps the duckling on the beach. Here Rumi refers to the illusionary self that created the fear of prison without a wall.

"A voice calls on our spirit,
not to wait anymore
Prepare to move
to the real home.

Your real home
your real birthplace."

The Painted Jackal

A Jackal slipped and fell on a paddle of paint. He splashed and rolled from side to side, covering his entire body with colorful paint. As he came off the paint, he noticed that different parts of his body were covered with different colors: His ride side was red, his left side was yellow, and his tail was white.

Turning his head from side to side, he started to see his beautiful body. He was mesmerized by his new look and beauty and paused to admire himself. He thought that he was now as beautiful and enchanting as a peacock. He arrogantly walked toward his friends to show off his dazzling color, bringing admiration and praise from them.

His friends were not impressed with Jackal's new look. One of his old friends said, "What have you done to your body with all these colors?"

Another friend said, "None of us are impressed with your new look. You lost your identity, and this arrogance and happiness will not last long."

The Jackal, still in love with his new look, said, "I am now a flower garden. Have you ever seen an idol of beauty like me? I want you to observe my grace and majesty and kneel before me."

The jackals were annoyed and irritated by his new look and arrogant attitude. They circled him, and one of the older jackals asked him. "If you are not a jackal now, what should we call you?"

"I am the exquisite and magnificent peacock."

The jackals laughed and asked him, "If you're a peacock, let us hear your piercing song."

"Oh, no, I can't sing."

His friends chuckled and walked away from the egotistic Jackal.

Moral of the story:

Rumi believed that a sense of false Identity is the barrier preventing us from joining the source and attaining true happiness. Attachment to wealth, fame, beauty, and physical appearance is the leading cause of false Identity. This attachment to materialism makes us selfish. Selfishness (Ego) and love both grow in the heart. When we fill our hearts with selfishness, there is no more room for love to grow inside our hearts, and as a result, there is not enough fuel to take us to the path of unification with the beloved.

"If you desire grace, lose your selfish self and taste the sweet essence."

"Your worst enemy is hiding within yourself; that enemy is your nafs or ego."

The Wise Goldsmith

A wise goldsmith had just opened his shop and started to sweep the floor as routine when the door opened, and an older man holding a bag entered the shop. "Good morning, my dear goldsmith. Sorry to bother you this early morning. Can I use your scale to weigh my gold scrapes?"

The goldsmith stopped brooming. "I don't have a small broom and sieve to give you."

The old man wrinkled his forehead, squinted, and with a louder voice, said, "I didn't ask for a broom or a sieve. I need your scale to weigh my fine gold."

The goldsmith said, "I am not deaf. I heard from you, and please leave. I don't have time for arguments this early in the morning. I need to take care of my business."

"Let me just borrow your scale." The older man repeated.

The wise goldsmith said, "I am not dumb. I know from experience you need a sieve and broom when you weigh your gold as fine as powder."

The older man shook his head. "I don't understand why you insist I need a broom and sieve. That has nothing to do with weighing my gold."

The goldsmith said, "To get the gold, you must deal with the dust first. With a slide shake in your hand, the entire bag could scatter on the floor and mix with the dirt. Then you ask me for a broom to sweep up the gold mixed with the dirt. Next, you will ask me for a sieve to separate dust from gold."

The older man sighed and left the shop.

Moral of the story:

If we want gold, we need to get rid of dust. Rumi compared dust to the illusionary self in these metaphors and gold to the true self. We cannot connect to our true selves until we eliminate *our egos.*

"The Ego is a curtain between humans and God."

"I long to escape my ego's prison and lose myself in you."

The Holy Sufi and The Death of His Sons

When A holy Sufi two young sons died, the entire neighborhood came to the mosque to mourn their beloved master's son's death. Everyone came, cried, and felt sorry for the death of two beautiful children.

The only person that didn't shed a tear was the Sufi himself. His devotees were puzzled over the indifference of a father burying his children. People were perplexed and wanted to know what had happened to their holy man. Weeks after the funeral, one of his followers approached him, "My dear Shaykh, forgive me for my intrusion into your personal life. People want to know why you remained so unfeeling about the passing of your two precious children?"

The Sufi listened carefully to the woman and leaned back against the wall. "As most of you know, I empathize with everyone, including animals. "

The devotees said, "That is what surprised your followers to see you care for everyone, but you didn't cry or even show any emotions on the death of your children."

The Sufi stopped fingering his *Tasebe* and leaned forward. "For those who know me, it shouldn't be a surprise. Dead is not gone forever. It is passing from one life to another. I see my children with the eyes of my heart all the time. I see they are playing joyfully. Sometimes they cry when they feel the separation between us. They are by my side all the time when I am awake.

Moral of the story:

The only reality that exists is the true self or divine consciousness. Divine consciousness entered our body with the first breath and left our body with the last breath. Death is the ultimate escape from the prison of the illusionary self.

"When you see my body is being carried away,

don't cry. I'm going nowhere.

I'm arriving at eternal love,

It seems like the end, but it is just the sunset."

It is Not as It Appears.

A grocer had an eloquently spoken parrot as his best friend and companion. The parrot was not just an ideal companion but also increased his profit by entertaining the customers and keeping an eye on the store to stop stealing. All customers admired the bird and continued coming to the store to talk with the parrot and learn what new words he had learned.

One day the grocer went home for lunch as usual and left the shop in the care of his trusted bird.

While he was away, a cat chased a mouse inside the shop, and the parrot was scared, jumping from one shelf to another and knocking off one almond oil bottle on the ground. The glass was scattered all over the floor, and oil spilled on the parrot's body and covered the floor.

The parrot, ashamed of his clumsiness, quietly perched on the corner of the store. A few minutes later, the grocer returned to his shop and found his shop in disarray. The grocer lost his temper and hit the bird on his head. The bird couldn't bear the shame and the pain; he shed all the feathers from his head and became completely bald.

He stopped talking. The grocer realized his mistake as fewer customers came to the store to shop. He also missed talking with his favorite friend. "How could I strike my best friend for something not his fault? I wished my hands were broken in pieces."

He tried to talk with the parrot, but the parrot sat quietly at the shop with his head down. He spoke with anyone who had a parrot to find a way for his parrot to talk again. He gave alms to any dervish passed by his shop. It seemed none of his efforts helped his bird to speak again.

One day a bald Dervish came to the shop. The bird went to the front of the shop and locked his stare on the bald head of the dervish. Before the Darwish walked away, the bird said, "Did you spill the almond oil too?"

The grocer was ecstatic that his parrot was talking again. The customers were amused at the parrot, who thought the bald Darwish suffered the same fate as he did. One of the customers gently patted the bird. "My lovely parrot, you shouldn't equate one action with another. One must not compare oneself to others and not judge everything from experience. Things are not identical, even if they appear identical on the surface."

Moral of the story:

Reality is not as it appears.

"This is not the reality.

Reality is behind the curtains.

In truth, we are not here.

This is our shadow."

"To see what can't be seen,

Give up your eyes and

 listen with your heart." Najim Mostamand

Prophet Mohammad's Valuable Advice

During the lifetime of the prophet Mohammad, people came to him for his advice and guidance. People spent months on the arduous journey to be in the company of the prophet and listen to his words of wisdom. Some came to him when encountering a specific family or business issue. Most felt the prophet would direct them to the right path and show them the way.

One day prophet finished talking with his followers when a man approached him. He waited until it was his turn. He was lost for words as he sat quietly before the prophet. It took the merchant a few moments to gather his taught and present his dilemma to the prophet. "My dear prophet, I am coming to you from a far distance for a problem that affects my life and my family. Even though I am supposed to be a merchant, I can no longer provide for my family."

The prophet listened to all sorts of problems from his followers, but his story puzzled him on how a merchant couldn't provide for his family. They are the wealthiest people in the country.

"I didn't understand. How could you be a merchant and unable to provide for your family? Please explain."

The merchant said, "I travel in a large caravan around the country for trade. But I lost in all the trades. It doesn't matter if I buy or sell. My trading partner takes advantage of me, and I cannot confront him."

Prophet Mohammad said, "You must confront your cheating partner, but be patient and wait at least three days before making any major decision."

The prophet sensed that he might not clarify himself, so he gave this example. "When you throw a piece of bread in front of a dog, he doesn't rush to eat the bread. He takes his time to smell the bread before he eats it. He uses his sense to make critical decisions. Then why should we use our minds to make important decisions? When you wait, you use all your senses to decide, not just your head. Waiting allows your feeling, which comes from your heart, to communicate with your head and come to a balanced, fair decision that benefits both sides."

The merchant was happy that he traveled this long distance to hear this valuable advice from the prophet.

Moral of the story:

Our decision should come both from the heart and from the mind. If we make all the decisions from our minds, they are not balanced and only benefit us. The mind is selfish and always asks, "What is in it for me." But the heart considers everyone's profit in a deal.

Bilal's Passing

Bilal was a devoted Muslim, a kind and compassionate man. Everyone in the town liked him and admired his hard work and devotion to needy people.

He aged prematurely, but he was not bitter about it. He was losing weight fast and couldn't leave his bed for the mosque.

His wife knew that time had arrived, "my dear Bilal, don't leave me. How can I live without you?"

Bilal said with a faint and broken voice, "Don't cry. It is time to rejoin my beloved. Death is a different stage of life."

When Bilal talked about death and joining the beloved, it seemed he was never sick. His face lit up.

His wife wiped her tears and said, "You will leave your family and enter a strange place."

"No, no, my dear, I leave this strange place and enter my eternal home where I came from."

Bilal spoke his last word and closed his eyes forever.

Moral of the story:

Dying is leaving the material world and joining the beloved. Death is a homecoming that should be celebrated, not mourned. The consciousness that occupies our body returns home to join the source.

If I am with you, The Desert is like a Paradise

Two lovers arrived at a colorful garden and sat beside each other close to a stream of rose bushes.

It was early morning, and no one else was in sight as far as they could see.

The young girl faced his lover, "You traveled everywhere and had seen many cities. Tell me what your favorite place was?"

"The best place in the world is where you are. Sitting close to you is my ultimate wish, and I am the happiest in your company."

The girl said, "What if it is in the middle of a hot desert?'

"If I am with you, the desert is Paradise for me."

The girl smiled, and they embraced each other.

Moral of the story:

The happiest place is in the company of the beloved.

"Your love raised my soul from the body to the sky,
And you lift me out of this world."

Guest Killer Mosque

There was a mosque in Rey, Persia, where all travelers stayed overnight when passing by the city. This mosque became famous among the townsman as the guest killer mosque, and it was for a good reason. In the past few months, any traveler who stayed overnight in the mosque was killed.

The residents of the city warned all strangers coming to the town. Most strangers listened to the warning and never slept in the mosque for the night. The townspeople were pleased that most travelers listened to their warning and avoided spending the night in the mosque.

But one day, a fearless traveler entered the city. People gathered around him, notified him about the haunted mosque, and advised him not to sleep there. Even a kind man offered him a room in his house to sleep in, but he declined.

The people warned him if he entered the mosque, he would be tortured and killed by an evil force in the mosque before midnight. He responded to the objection of the people gathered by the mosque door. "My body has no value. It is my spirit that is priceless. I am tired of this life and have no fear of death. If I lose my life tonight, then I achieved my purpose."

The people concluded that their effort to discourage him from spending overnight in the mosque was fruitless, and they dispersed and went home.

After the people left, the traveler entered the mosque and closed the heavy, engraved wooden door behind him. He looked around the mosque and sat leaning against the wall on the corner. The fear of dying never entered his mind. Before it turned dark, he lit a half-burned candle, opened his bag, and ate a small piece of the bread. Before midnight the candle went out, and the mosque became pitch black dark.

It was almost midnight, he thought; he did not see or hear any devil's voice. He was convinced that it was just a rumor or that the townsman told the story for travelers not to stay in the mosque. He was drowning in his thought and forgot about the devil when a piercing voice broke his thought. "I will take your life by midnight."

Any other person would have a heart attack hearing this loud fearful voice, but not this brave traveler.

He stood at the center of the mosque and yelled back. "For the faithless, your voice is the drum of death. But your voice is a celebration drum for those who believe in God. Here I am. I have nothing to lose but everything to gain. Come and take me."

Those words broke the mosque's spell. The mosque ceiling cracked open, and the glittering coins of gold came down like a flowing river. The gold coins covered the mosque's colorful mosaic.

The fearless traveler is still in awe, not believing his eyes. He looked around the mosque and found an empty bag. He filled the bag with gold coins and lived happily for the rest of his life.

Moral of the story:

Leaving a familiar place and entering an unknown world is scary. We are so used to our illusionary self-environments, believing it is our natural world, and we don't leave this world to enter a world that is so strange to us.

Not knowing that the new world is our true reality where we can access the wisdom of the heart that can bring us happiness and genuine wisdom. That place is the ultimate reality. Our current world is a collection of images of our thoughts from real and unreal events in our life. Get out of this prison and enter the world of your true self. You have the key in your pocket.

"Light of spirit God sends trials of suffering and pain so the gold of the Spirit may manifest. Surrender."

The Tanner in The Perfume Bazaar

A Tanner worked long hours in his shop to finish the many orders he had received in the past few days. One day he worked so hard that by the end of the day, he had no energy to continue his work. He just wanted to go home, have a bite, and go to bed. He closed his shop and walked toward his home. He was so drained that it made him take a wrong turn, ending at the perfume bazaar.

He knew that he was lost. Het approached a perfume shop to ask for directions when the smell of fragrance overwhelmed him and put his head in a spin. He fainted and passed out on the floor. People gathered around his lifeless body, trying to help.

One rubbed his chest, another man through rose water on his face. A wise man saw the commotion, and he went inside his shop and mixed some herbs with his assistant's help, raised the tanner's head, and put a few spoons table of herbs inside his mouth. Another townsman checked his pulse. It seemed that nothing helped, and the lifeless body of the tanner didn't move.

Soon they knew who this man was, and most people knew his famous brother; a man ran and notified his brother. His brother came to the scene and collected dog feces on his way to the perfume bazaar. After he arrived, he pushed the people away and got closer to his brother.

The bystanders told him they used many things, but none helped his brother.

He said, "If we know the illness, it is easy to find the cure—From dawn to dusk, my brother works in a tannery where the smell is unbearable for others, but my brother only knows that smell and cannot tolerate the strange smell of perfume. He is not to it. He became sick because he was exposed to an unfamiliar scent of perfume. All of his body is adapted to foul smell. The cure for my brother is the dog feces smell, not the rose water."

He opened the bag and shoved the dog feces into his brother's nose. He let him breathe on the foul smell for a few minutes. Soon his brother opened his eyes and took a deep breath. The people helped him stand. After a few minutes, he walked home with his brother.

Moral of the story:

Most of the time, we fear pain and suffering, trying to escape it, not realizing that pain and suffering are trying to send us a message. We should not complain about the pain and suffering and instead try to know the news behind our pain and suffering.

"The cure for the pain is in pain.

Suffering is a gift, in its hidden mercy."

Mud Eater

A disease with no known cure or cause affected many people in a small town in Persia. People with this sickness were addicted to eating mud with no self-control. They nibbled on the smallest size of mud where they could find.

One day a mud eater entered a grocery store to purchase sugar. The merchant soon became aware of the person's addiction and tried to exploit him. He put some weights made of mud on the scale and said, "You know this weight is very accurate, and I made them from the mud. Let me go in the back and bring your sugar."

The shopkeeper walked to the back of his shop and hid behind a curtain, watching the mud eater. The man was happy when the shopkeeper left. He picked up one of the mud weights from the scale and smelled it.

He couldn't control himself and took a few small bites from the mud weight, thinking he had cheated the merchant by eating his mud weight. The shopkeeper watching him in hiding took his time, allowing the man to eat as much of his weight as he wanted. After a few more minutes, the shopkeeper returns with a bag of sugar in his hand. He was happy that he gave less sugar to the man as he had already eaten half of the weight.

The mud eater paid the shopkeeper and left the store with half the sugar he had paid for. He was happy that he ate some mud without paying for it, not knowing that he had lost half of his sugar.

Moral of the story:

Attachment to materialism is like an addiction; it hurts you without knowing it—attachment to materialism creates a sense of false identity, the ego, which is incompatible with love. The ego prevents you from connecting with your true self.

The Dervish and The Sufi Master

On a cold winter night, a dervish went to bed early. In his dream, he saw himself in the company of a Sufi teacher. He quickly took advantage of this opportunity and learned from the Sufi master. He asked the Sufi to advise him on how to live without working hard or creating bad karma.

The Sufi told him about a magical mountain in a faraway land where he could find all sorts of fruit. The trees bear fruit year-round; all the fruit is within reach, and you don't need to climb the tree to get the fruit.

Without much effort, the young Dervish found this magical mountain. He saw all sorts of abundant trees full of fruit. He spent most of the time under the tree, getting up only to pick some fruit for breakfast, lunch, and dinner. One day he walked to a nearby stream to wash. As he removed his coat, he found two coins he had sewed in his sleeve long ago. While he recovered the coins, he saw an older man with a bent back carrying a stack of firewood. He immediately thought he no longer needed the coins and would give them as alms to this poor older man to buy food to nourish himself.

The young Dervish was unaware that this older man was the highest Sufi Master who could read other people's thoughts. By this time, the master Sufi had reached where the young Dervish stood. He was offended by what the Dervish thought of him. He put the stack of firewood on the ground and kneeled Infront of them, "O, my almighty, use your divine power to turn this firewood into gold!"

In an instant, the firewood turned into gold. The Dervish froze in his place and couldn't move.

After a few minutes, the master dervish raised his hand to the sky, "O, my beloved, for the sake of your lover, please turn this gold to its original form."

Again, in an instant, the gold turned to firewood. The master Sufi started walking back to the town, hoping he taught a lesson to this young Dervish not to underestimate a working man's desire to earn money instead of waiting for a handout.

Moral of the story:

Earn your money. Don't wait for a handout. We all can perform something. We need to find what it is that we are made for it.

A community cannot progress if all its members don't take part in building it. We must not take advantage of others by letting everyone work, and we receive the handout. Every capable person should contribute to the community's advances to grow and prosper. If we can do any work, we shouldn't wait for help. Obviously, in each community, some people need help. We should show compassion and kindness to those who genuinely need help and confront those who want to take advantage of others by making excuses because anyone can do something good. It doesn't matter how big or small.

In this story, the older man tries to teach the young Darwish that he doesn't want a handout, even if it is gold. He still can earn his money by gathering wood.

And anyone with a desire to work could even turn firewood into gold.

"Everyone has been made for a specific work, and the desire for that particular work has been put in every heart."

Giving up The Kingdom

Ibrahim, the ruler of Balkh, was a powerful and fair king. His people admired and loved him. He was famous for helping people experiencing poverty.

One night he was awakened by a loud voice on his roof. He thought, who dared to come to the palace with the guards protecting the castle in all the gates? He waited a few more minutes, but the rumbling on the roof never stopped. He thought an enemy soldier might invade his kingdom, and the guard tried to notify him.

With a loud voice, he walked to the window and yelled, "Who is there this late at night?"

A group of men voice, responded, "It is us."

The king said, "What are you looking for?"

The men said, "We are chasing the camels."

The king became angry and said, "What an idiot. Why does someone chase the camels on the roof?"

The men responded, "For the same reason, you are chasing the God from your palace."

He didn't know what to say when Ibrahim heard the men respond. He couldn't sleep that night. In the morning, he left the palace with only his outfit, not taking anything from the castle.

Moral of the story:

"The more awake we are to the material world, the more we are asleep to our true self."

Rumi used the palace metaphor for the material world and illusionary self in this tale. We can't join the beloved while attached to materialism. We need to destroy our ego to join the beloved. The ego is the veil that separates us from our true selves.

"Kill the cow of your ego so that your inner spirit comes to life and attain true awareness."

The Garden of Inner Beauty

A dervish left his home early on a sunny morning to run long overdue errands. But as usual, he started his morning by going to the city garden in the town's center. The lush garden was full of fruit trees and rose bushes. A small stream runs through the park, and the birds chirp in the morning and fly from one fruit tree to another. Humongous willow trees, green bushes, and flowers covered the garden.

The dervish walked inside the garden and sat quietly by the stream under a willow tree. He closed his eyes and started his meditation.

A young man who was also enjoying the freshness of the garden passed by the dervish, and he thought the dervish had fallen asleep. Without consideration for his privacy, he approached the dervish and said, "Why are you sleeping here and not taking advantage of the beauty that God created here in this garden for us to enjoy and admire him? You sin by not seeing the beauty that God created."

The dervish raised his head and was not happy with the intrusion of this young man, "the beauty inside you is the beauty of God's glory; the outside is a mere manifestation of your inside beauty."

The dervish closed his eyes again and continued with his meditation.

Moral of the story:

What we can find outside us cannot be compared to what we can find inside us. We can only find True beauty and happiness inside our hearts.

"Pull the thorn of life out of the heart! Fast! You will find thousands of rose gardens in yourself when you do."

The Size of The Turban

A teacher lived and taught in a city where the size of the turban indicated a man's stature and knowledge. The teacher had no wealth or high degree to receive the highest name and respect from his associate, students, and townspeople.

To satisfy his hunger for name and respect, he devised an idea to gradually increase the size of his turban to earn the respect he desired. He started collecting cotton and leftover clothes from the shops and stuffed them in his turban. After a few months, the size of the turban grew large enough to give him the appearance of a Valor and an accomplished man.

At the time, many thought people hid their money and jewelry in turbans to keep them safe.

One morning, the teacher was walking toward the school, thinking of his lecture today, when a thief appeared from nowhere, grabbed his turban, and ran. From the size of the turban, the thief was very happy that he would be rich.

 It took a few minutes for the teacher to realize what had happened. He ran after the thief and shouted, "Stop and look. There is no real money or jewelry inside the turban. You achieved nothing."

The thief stopped running, looked inside the turban, and found useless pieces of cotton and cloth. He threw away the turban and started running again.

The teacher picked up his turban and thought, "I achieved nothing either." He threw the cotton and pieces of cloth away, rearranged the turban back to its original size, and continued his walk toward the school.

Moral of the story:

We think that wealth, fame, and knowledge bring us respect and happiness, unaware that they can hurt us more than they can help us.

"Don't be enchanted with the outside world. It is all empty inside. Look inside yourself and find real gold."

Leadership is About the Strength of the Heart.

Prophet Mohammad was looking for a general to lead his new army. After interviewing many generals and considering all the qualities a leader should have, he hired a young soldier as his new general to lead his army to victory.

The young general didn't fight in many wars and never had led an army of such size. But prophet Mohammad was attracted to his wisdom and quick to decide under tremendous stressful and challenging times. Prophet Muhammad was sure the young general would make a wise decision during the battle. The young man participated in many wars alongside the prophet Mohammad but had no rule in decision-making about the battle.

The young man also had close ties with the prophet while traveling and knew he could trust the young man with his life. Mohammad was aware of the man's wisdom and the strength of his heart.

His decision brought a lot of resentment and jealousy from the older general with much experience with war. Many of these generals fought alongside the prophet and conquered many cities.

An older general with a thick grey beard couldn't hide his feelings anymore; he approached the prophet and said, "Our greater messenger. I learned your decision to make an inexperienced young man your general. We have many generals in the army with leadership qualities to choose as generals instead of a young man who never had any leadership rule in our battles. You must choose an older man who fought battles and know how to lead and win a war."

Mohammad was aware that his decision brought an uproar among more experienced older generals, but he knew he had made the right decision. He put his hand on the shoulder of his general and said, "My dear friend, you're mistaken not to look into the hidden quality of a person to lead our large army. Experience and knowledge are good but not essential qualities for a leadership position.

I have accomplished generals, but the heart of many of them are tainted with ego, jealousy, and resentment. The young man has an untainted heart critical for making quick decisions during a battle. Don't just look at his appearance as a qualifying factor. Look in the strength of his heart which is hidden from your sight. I see the strength of the heart as the most qualified factor for a general to lead our army to victory.

The young man I chose to lead the army has a pearl of innate wisdom far better than having battle experience.

He can see things clearly and make judgments with his heart and mind that could save lives on both armies in a battle while winning the war with the least casualties possible."

The older general knew he could trust the prophet's decisions; this time, it was no exception.

Moral of the story:

"Our greatest strength lies in the gentleness and tenderness of our hearts."

We should not judge people based on their appearance. We should make decisions with the cleverness of our minds and the intuitive wisdom of our hearts. Making decisions with heart and the mind's input is fair and balanced for all parties involved. Decisions made only by the mind are not balanced, as the mind is selfish and only makes decisions to benefit itself.

Three Fish

Three fish lived all their lives in a clear pond close to the mountain by a fast-flowing stream. One day a couple of men decided to go to the hill and have a picnic. They knew the stream and the pond, hoping to catch fish for lunch. As they got to the pond, they stood silent to see if there were any fish. Soon they saw three good-sized fish and started preparing their net.

One of the most intelligent fish soon realized what was happening. He knew that he needed to come up with a decision to save his life soon. He thought if he consulted his friends, they would go against his decision, as they had lived all their lives in the pond, and here they felt safe and didn't want to go to an unfamiliar place.

He decided to leave the pond without any hesitation. With a leap of faith, he gathered all his strength and jumped out of the pond to the stream. The fast-flowing stream took him to the sea, where he swam freely without being forced to circle the pond. He felt the joy of freedom and swam in the vast warm water of the ocean without any restriction. He knew that his fear of the unknown would soon disappear, and he was ecstatic about his decision to free himself while feeling sorry for his friends.

He hoped his friends realized their demise and escaped to the ocean, where they could find freedom and happiness.

The second fish knew not much time left to save his life. He thought if he had played dead, the men wouldn't eat a dead fish and might throw him away.

He pretended to be dead, and the pond ripple floated it around. One man said, "Let us throw away the dead fish. We all get sick if we eat it."

He grabbed the fish and threw it away. The fish jumped up and down, rolled to the stream, and floated to the safety of the ocean.

There was not much time left for the third fish to escape. He waited too long, hoping for a miracle, but soon he saw himself inside the net, and there was no chance of running. He wished he had followed his friend and found a way to escape.

Soon the men had delicious fish cooked on the open fire.

Moral of the story:

"It is your road and yours alone. Someone might walk with you, but no one walks it for you."

It is tough to leave our familiar place, the illusionary self. We feel safe where we have lived most of our lives. Separating from the illusionary self needs courage and preparation. Others can help you, but no one makes the journey for you. The longer you stay in your illusionary home, the more you suffer from your inability to leave. The ones who find the courage to leave the illusionary world will find true peace and happiness, joining their true self.

Saving a Servant's Life

The king was furious when he heard about one of his servants' mistakes. He summoned the servant to his chamber to punish him for his crime. After a brief discussion, the King made his decision. When the other workers became aware that the servant received death punishment from the king, nobody interfered with the king's decision, as they knew that only the most trusted minister, Emad, could save the servant's life.

Emad came to the king and asked him to forgive the servant as it was the first time he had committed a crime since he went to the palace twenty years ago. The king listened to his trusted minister and forgave the servant.

Emad told the servant, "Go to your quadrant, and don't come to the palace until the king's anger subsides."

The palace workers noticed that the servant's attitude toward Emad changed. He complained about Emad to other servants. He avoided the minister and didn't greet him when they crossed paths at the palace.

The other servant didn't understand him and was puzzled why his attitude changed toward the minister who saved his life.

One day a close friend of the servant asks him, "Why do you disrespect the man who saved your life?"

"I didn't ask Emad to save my life. My life didn't belong to him. My life belongs to the king, who can only decide when to take my life. I wanted to become nothing in front of the king. Emad took that chance away from me."

Moral of the story:

Rumi used metaphor in this story to show the need to kill *Nafs*, the illusionary self, to join the world of divinity within, the true self. King is a metaphor for the beloved, and the servant is the illusionary self that must die. The minister is the attachment to the material, preventing us from destroying the illusionary self.

Once we destroy the illusionary self, we can join the beloved, authentic self, divinity within.

The Calligraphy

One day a group of ants left their colony and made a left turn instead of their usual route to go straight. Soon they found themselves on a white paper that someone was writing. One of the younger ants who didn't see the fingers holding the pen said, "Look at this incredible shape that the pen is creating."

Another ant said, "The fingers holding the pen create this beauty."

Another ant got into the conversation. "You are all wrong. It is the arms that create these amazing shapes and designs."

The ants' leader tried to settle the argument, got into conversation, and said, "A superior energy force creates these designs and shapes. Matter cannot create these designs or form, as the matter will be destroyed during times, but energy or the force that is the universal consciousness is the creator of the eternal design."

The ants continued their walk and found the right path to get the leaves.

Moral of the story:

There is an energy template behind any creation in the universe. This energy is the life force, universal consciousness, source, spirit, or God. The name does not change the concept. We give it a name based on our beliefs and upbringing.

The energy template for our body already exists, and our physical body is made from all the details of that template. This life force or universal intelligence designed everything to make the trillions of cells in our body work harmoniously for us to exist. The existence of life without this force energy is inconceivable. Everything in our physical world is a manifestation of this energy template.

"If everything in the universe disappears, we have the template to bring it back to its original form."

The Beauty of a Peacock

A man was walking to his farmhouse when he saw a peacock in the distance. First, he couldn't believe his eyes as he had never seen a peacock passing this route in all these years. As he got closer, he knew that he was not mistaken. He was first mesmerized by the beauty of the peacock, but then he noticed that the peacock angrily picked up his feathers with his beak, spitting them as far as he could. The man couldn't believe his eyes. He carefully approached the peacock and said,

"Why pick up your feathers one by one? Don't you know how people admire you for your beautiful feathers? The king gives you a special place to admire your beauty in his palace. People use your beautiful feathers to bookmark their books; Without these beautiful feathers, you are nobody. You don't get any admiration."

The peacock patiently waited for the man to finish his talk. He spat the feather toward the man, saying, "You humans are distracted with superficial beauty. These feathers are the reason for my sorrow and pain. The hunters can spot me from miles away. I cannot protect myself because of these feathers. I want to roam anywhere without fear of being shot and killed. These feathers are the cause of my egotism that brought me so much pain. Now is the time to get rid of myself from superficial beauty for the people to see my real beauty."

The peacock continued picking his feathers. The man learned a valuable lesson from his encounter with this unique creature.

Moral of the story:

We are attached to beauty and materialism, thinking it brings us happiness and success. But we realized it all had been a mirage once we were there. False identity is the source of our unhappiness. Our beauty or wealth attracts the wrong people, who are only interested in our beauty and wealth. Keeping these types of people in our company hurts us, and we never get to find true friends to like us for the person we are, not for the person we appear to be.

Laila and Majnun

Laila and Majnun are epic stories in Persian literature. It captured the imagination of millions for centuries. Majnun was in Love with Laila, but their union never materialized, as their family never agreed.

Majnun fell ill from Laila's separation and stopped eating. He started walking purposelessly on the street and became the subject of ridicule by villagers. His illness became severe, and one of his friends took him to a medicine man, who immediately diagnosed his sickness and told his friend that the only cure for Majnun was to bleed him. His blood is infected, and he will die if we don't drain his blood.

Majnun was lying down unconscious and barely understood the conversation's subject. The assistant for the medicine man prepared the razor and a pan with enough cloth to clean the blood. As he was ready to cut his arm for the blood to come out, Majnun pulled his arm back. "Leave me alone."

The medicine man said, "If I don't drain your blood, you won't survive tonight."

With a faint voice, Majnun said, "Don't harm her!"

"I am another you. You are another me."

The medicine man taught that he had a high fever, and his words didn't make sense. He asked his friend to convince Majnun to let him cut his arm to draw the blood.

With a calming voice, his friend lowered his head and whispered, "You are the bravest man I have ever known. Why are you afraid of a cut on your arm?"

Majnun opened his mouth to say something but didn't have the energy to push the words out. With a closed eye, he wet his lips and said, "I am not afraid. My body doesn't exist anymore. My Love takes over my entire body for Laila. I am worried he might cut her simultaneously if he cuts my arm. We are both one now. There are no longer two bodies; only one exists."

"If I love myself, I love you.

If I love you, I love myself."

Moral of the story:

"Your spirit is mingled with mine. What touches you touches me."

There is no "I" when people are in true Love. I disappear to the true Love of our beloved. In true Love, two bodies become one; only "You" can exist. There is no room for duality when we dissolve ourselves in the Love of our beloved.

"The minute I heard my love story,

I started looking for you, not knowing

How blind I was.

Lovers don't finally meet somewhere.

They're in each other all along."

Treasure in Egypt

In Baghdad, a man inherited a fortune from his rich dad, a famous merchant. But the son had no experience making good deals and expanding his inherited wealth. He made many mistakes and lost all the money he inherited from his dad. He was almost left homeless. He worked hard to establish his name and regain his wealth but failed. He gave up, regretted his mistake, and lost his passion for life.

One night he dreamed of a treasure hidden in Egypt in a basement. He woke up strangely, trying to make sense of his sleep. Desperate to become wealthy again, he decided to go to Egypt to search for treasure. He gathered some of his belonging and started his long and arduous journey with the first caravan traveling to Egypt.

After a month of traveling, he finally arrived in Egypt. He didn't have any relatives or friends in Egypt and did not have money to stay in a guest house. He found a place in the main bazaar and settled on a street corner. He was cold and hungry but couldn't bring himself to bag for food or money.

Lately, there has been a robbery in this city. The police chief is under much pressure from the mayor to catch the culprit. They increased their presence in all parts of the city. One night they came across this man from Baghdad sitting at the corner of the street. When the police approached him, they took him into custody and beat him to confess his crime. He said,

"I am not from Egypt. I just came to this city to find a hidden treasure."

He told his story to the police. The police felt sorry for him and said, "I don't think you are a thief, but I think you are not smart. How could you travel this far to search for a treasure in Egypt based on your dream? I also once dreamed that a treasure was hidden in Mr. Razwan's basement. Should I have traveled to Baghdad to find the treasure?"

Once he heard his name, he was ecstatic, and the next day he started his long journey back to Baghdad, wondering why he had trouble finding the treasure already in his house.

Moral of the story:

We are mainly unhappy because we are unaware of the treasure hidden inside us. We always look for glory and happiness outside us without knowing it has been with us all this time.

"Stop acting so small. You are the universe in ecstatic motion."

Author's Note

From an early age, my fascination with Rumi's enchanting tales and poetry unwittingly ignited a passion for his works. I found myself drawn to their profound depth and imaginative narratives, embarking on a unique journey of interpretation shaped by my upbringing and experiences. I humbly acknowledge my interpretation of Rumi's stories and poems is subjective, understanding that each individual may interpret them differently. After all, the heart of moral stories lies in the lessons they convey, regardless of the specific moral communicated.

A charismatic storyteller, well-versed in Persian literature, became a pivotal figure in my journey. His animated delivery and expressive gestures breathed life into the narratives, captivating our hearts as if we were immersed in an enthralling TV show. Thursday nights became cherished moments, often past midnight, as we absorbed meaningful stories and their valuable teachings.

In time, we discovered our storyteller was a retired literature teacher and an expert in *Masnavi*, Rumi's notable work. Nearly all the stories he shared derived from this profound masterpiece. My father, introducing me to Rumi at a tender age, profoundly influenced my life's trajectory. Rumi's teachings reassured me that my beliefs were not solitary. They instilled the confidence to pursue a purposeful life and reminded me to sing like a bird, regardless of who listens or overlooks.

As my love for Rumi's poetry blossomed, I delved deeper into his philosophy of finding God within. Despite living in a society where many religious individuals reject such notions, I found myself often at odds with prevailing norms. Rumi's poetic wisdom resonated deeply with me, fueling my interpretation of his poetry through my early education in Rumi's native Afghanistan.

Having studied *Masnavi* and Rumi's poetry in its original Persian language, I aimed to preserve the essence of Rumi's verses in my translations. Translating metaphor-laden and symbol-rich poetry inevitably falls short of capturing its complete beauty. Still, a fundamental understanding of Rumi's philosophy allows us to appreciate his poetic genius even in translated versions.

Rumi's teaching stories in *Masnavi* unveil the intricacies of the universe and life itself. Armed with a profound understanding of Rumi's perspectives on life, the universe, and our existence, these stories possess the potential to enact profound changes within us. Rumi described *Masnavi* as the root of religion and the explainer of the Quran. To truly grasp the essence of his poetry, we must consider the influence of Rumi's upbringing, culture, and religion, inseparable from his poetic narrative. Many English translations fail to convey this integral aspect, diluting Rumi's teachings.

With unwavering dedication, I sought to translate Rumi's poetry literally, ensuring its poetic essence and true meaning remained intact while respecting Rumi's beliefs, culture, and religion. Regrettably, numerous books have distorted Rumi's beliefs, teachings, and poetry, often due to ignorance or unfamiliarity with the environment in which Rumi thrived. The true meaning of Rumi's poetry can become lost in translation, as only a limited number of his poems have been directly translated from Farsi, his native language.

As a child, I enjoyed hearing *Masnavi*'s stories in Farsi, memorizing and immersing myself in Rumi's verses. Being from the same country and speaking the same language offered me a unique advantage in preserving the essence of Rumi's poetry during translation. Nevertheless, both English and Farsi literature have linguistic limitations, with specific words in Rumi's poetry lacking direct synonyms. Despite these challenges, I endeavored to capture the essence of Rumi's poetry, offering readers a translation that remains faithful to its poetic resonance.

Thank you for choosing to read my book. I hope you enjoyed it and found it valuable. If you did, I would be honored if you could take a few moments to leave an honest review on Amazon. Your feedback will help other readers discover the book and decide if it fits them.

https://www.amazon.com/dp/B0BXK5MW5G

If you enjoyed this book, I encourage you to check my other works by clicking the link below. I'm passionate about writing and strive to provide value to my readers in every piece of work that I produce.

https://www.amazon.com/stores/Dr.-Farid-Mostamand/author/B09FZY8MD3?ref=ap_rdr&store_ref=ap_rdr&isDramIntegrated=true&shoppingPortalEnabled=true

Once again, thank you for your support, and I look forward to hearing your thoughts on the book.

Best regards,

Farid Mostamand

Shrine of Rumi, Konya, Turkey, 2022

FOREWORD

The title "Covenant for Rookies: Have You Ever Asked God Why?" is in no way derogatory to anyone, by any means. I originally wanted to title it "Covenant 4 Dummies" but could not secure permission to do so. And even that title might appear derogatory. The point of this book is to break down all the legal and technical ins and outs of our covenant with God, and to present the covenant in layman's terms, for all of us regular folks. No matter whether you are a rookie who's new to the covenant or whether you've been part of the family for ninety years, my prayer is that this book will bless you and assist you in better understanding all the benefits of the covenant God started with Abraham and finished with Christ.

So BUCKLE UP...and begin to see your covenant in a whole new way, enjoying all the benefits God went to great lengths to make available to you.

Boo Yah!
Andrew

Andrew D. Wittman
The Warrior Monk
www.thewarriormonk.org

INTRODUCTION

This book is probably going to be unlike any other book that you have ever read. Andrew Wittman takes you on an in-depth journey to the heart of Scripture to get answers to the most important question you can ask of God: "Why?" The Bible does provide answers to many questions. However, because those answers are often hidden in obscure places, many people find the Bible to be intimidating and confusing. If you agree with the previous statement, then this book will really help you in your search for answers. "Covenant for Rookies: Have You Ever Asked God Why?" is meant to serve as a road map or trail guide through the Bible. I recommend that you read this book with your Bible in hand. Don't just take Andrew's word for it, but let your faith rest on the Scripture.

"Covenant for Rookies: Have You Ever Asked God Why?" is a help for Christians from all backgrounds and denominations. And it may very well discuss certain ideas that you have never before been taught in church. Some of the contents may directly challenge what you have been taught or have always believed. As you have probably never met Andrew, allow me to share a few insights into what he believes and how he views the Bible.

1. God is good, and His Word is true. Regardless of background of denomination, we should all be able to agree with those statements. If you don't agree with either of them, then this book may not be for you.

2. The Bible is the final authority of the Christian faith here on earth. It is also a legal document, and God wrote what is inside for our instruction.

3. The Bible is the most unique book ever written, because it was God's Word spoken to men who wrote His words down. Obviously, God could not dump the entire truth on one man or even several of them. So He used many different people to tell many different accounts. With this history in mind, the Bible was not just meant to be read in chronological order like every other book in the world. God revealed something different to each person who had a role in writing the books of the Bible. And God wasn't the one that changed from book to book, but rather different sides of His character were revealed to different men like Moses, David, Solomon, Luke, John, Peter, and Paul. And if we interpret the verses in the Bible through the filter of God's character, we will find that the many different verses in many different books written by many different people all seem to fit together. Some in the theological world may disagree. But when applying the filter of God's character to all Scripture, you will find that taking God out of context is impossible, because His Word is always true.

4. The Bible was not written in modern-day or sixteenth-century English. The Old Testament was written in Hebrew and Aramaic, and the New Testament in Greek. In many ways, the English translation falls way short in delivering the true meaning of God's Word. I strongly recommend that you visit www.e-sword.net and download e-sword to your PC before beginning this book. (E-sword is an electronic Bible that shows the original Hebrew or Greek text for every English word used in the Bible, and it is completely free to download.) For example, the word "hope" in modern-day English usually refers to the act of simply wishing for something to occur. However, in Greek, the word "hope" means to have confidence or a confident expectation. The difference is subtle, but can you see it? That word is just one example, and there are many, many more. So hurry up and download e-sword before you turn another page!

5. Asking God "Why?" is okay. One of the benefits of believing on Jesus is that we get to have a one-on-one relationship with the Creator of the

universe. Not only is that thought exciting, but it can also be pretty intimidating. But the truth is that He desires to have a perfect "father-child" relationship with each one of us, and not the father-child relationship where He is constantly telling us what to do and not do. He wants to have the healthy relationship with you that you hopefully have with your earthly father or grandfather as a full-grown adult. As an adult, if your father or grandfather does something that you don't understand, you are probably going to ask him "Why?" Your relationship with your heavenly Father should be no different. He wants to give you answers to your questions so that you can have more confidence (hope) in Him.

6. Be open to new ideas that you find supported in the Bible. When Andrew was twelve years old, he decided that if something was in the Bible, he would believe it: end of story. You may or may not agree with him on that point. But I would encourage you to embrace the new ideas brought forth in *Covenant for Rookies: Have You Ever Asked*

God Why? Jesus spoke about how no one would put new wine into old wineskins because they would break and fall apart. New wine must be put into new wineskins. Jesus taught in parables because the message He brought was so cutting edge, so controversial, and so completely contrary to the religious teachings of the day. Parables were a way for Jesus to explain the seemingly complex in a simple context that the people could understand. But those who did hear Jesus required a new mindset in order to accept and believe Him. Just keep this thought in mind throughout this book: new cannot be put into old. What is new can only be put into something new. And if the old was best, we would have no need for the new.

I sincerely hope that this book blesses you in multiple ways. I am confident that you will find answers to questions that you may have been asking or have been afraid to ask for a long time. My one final suggestion would be just to keep reading. If you come across an idea that seems crazy, just put the book on your shelf for a while, and keep going. Now, buckle up and enjoy the ride!

Doug Brown

CEO, Perpetual Equity LLC

CHAPTER 1

What's a Covenant?

When I was in the grocery store yesterday with my wife, right there at the checkout counter I saw two little booklets called *Gambling for Dummies®* and *Poker for Dummies®*. The point of these guidebooks was to clue in those of us who don't know anything about gambling or poker, and to do so in a way that's easy to comprehend so that we can make practical use of the information contained within the pages. I'm sure you've seen or at least heard of the enormous selection of these kinds of "how to understand difficult subjects by having it explained in terms that regular folks can get" books like *Computers for Knuckleheads,*

and *Networking for Dingbats* and *All Kinds of Everything for Idiots,* etc. But there in the grocery store checkout line, the Lord began to speak to me about breaking down our covenant with Him in terms that we can all understand.

The Bible is a legal document, and if you have ever seen any legal documents or contracts, hoo-buddy, you have to untangle the language to figure out what's going on there. That legal lingo gives Congress a lot of problems up there on Capitol Hill, because all those elected officials fight over what the words mean, and what order the words should go, and how big to make those words so that the voters think they're really smart. As a result, no one can understand what the law really is, or what it's really saying, except for lawyers who also happen to specialize in that particular area of law. And the Bible is a legal document, a contract, written in a way that is legally binding. If you've ever had trouble understanding the Bible, relax. You're not the only one; don't take it personally. Just keep reading, and everything should begin to make sense.

Let's begin in the book of Hebrews, chapter 8 and verse 6. Quick note: If you're like me, you skip through the Scripture quotations when you read these types of books and jump ahead to see what the cat writing has to say about it. Well...DON'T! Read the Scripture verses; in fact, grab a Bible and look up the verses and read them out of the Bible for yourself. Look and see that these aren't a man's words, not some preacher's words, not Andrew's words: they are GOD'S WORDS! Oh, one more thing—I usually use the King James Version of the Bible because it's literal and NOT WATERED DOWN. No offense to the new-fangled versions, as I occasionally use the Amplified Bible for the sake of time in untangling the King James English in some passages. But newer versions just tend to water down the legal document known to us as the HOLY BIBLE, and I want the high-octane stuff. With the King James Version, you can take a Strong's Concordance and match up the original Hebrew and Greek with the English word for word. And because most folks are not perfectly fluent in Hebrew and Greek, that study is as close as non-linguists can get to actually seeing how God gave the Scripture to the original writers.

Let's jump into it:

But now hath he [Jesus] obtained a more excellent ministry, by how much also he is the mediator of a better covenant, which was established upon better promises. For if that first covenant had been faultless, then should no place have been sought for the second. In that he saith, A new covenant, he hath made the first old. Now that which decayeth and waxeth old is ready to vanish away.

Hebrews 8:6-7, 13

In the verses above, we see the word "covenant" used quite a bit. In the original Greek language, the word "covenant" could also be translated "testament." So, we have a new testament or a new covenant and an old testament or an old covenant. The covenant is the Word of God, or we could say that the Bible is our covenant. Don't get scared when you hear the word "covenant." I realize that it's a legal term and all, but God, in His mercy to us regular Joes, has boiled it down to three words. That's right, all that the covenant entails, the entire thing, the whole kit and caboodle, all that belongs to us, fits into three, little, simple words, and I'll tell you what the three words are in a minute. Wouldn't it be nice if the IRS would boil down the entire tax code into three, little, simple words? We all know that condensing the tax code is impossible; so you may be having a hard time believing me about boiling down the entire covenant into three words. Just hang in there, and we'll get to it. But first, let's learn a little bit about what a covenant life is, or living a life inside the covenant.

We have established that the Word of God is the covenant. Large numbers of Christians think of their relationship with God as a list of **DOs**, a bunch of behaviors that we have to **DO,** like Saturday morning chores. To most Christians, the Bible is a checklist of **DOs**, and doing the checklist, well, that'll make God like us better. If we **DO** all the **DO's** we're supposed to **DO**, God will be pleased, right?

An even larger number of folks are on "the outside", people that have never been "saved". They look at God's Word and think that it is a list of **DON'Ts**: "God just **DON'T** want me to do this and He **DON'T** want me to do that." We could sum up the **DON'Ts** like this: "Don't cuss, drink, smoke, or chew, or run around with those who do." That list of **DON'Ts** is pretty exhaustive. And what we ALL (both the **DO's** and the **DON'Ts**) are thinking is that God is out to take away all our fun. The vast majority of people on this planet think that the Bible should actually be titled *God's Really Big and Comprehensive List of **DO's** and **DON'Ts***.

But the Bible is not at all what we imagine. Our thinking about the Bible and God is completely wrong, because we have been taught religion, not the covenant. What the covenant is, what the covenant does, and what God commands us to do and not to do, are merely a set of boundaries or markers, a fence line. Inside the boundaries of the covenant, you can literally have heaven on earth.

When I was growing up, I would watch a TV show called *Bonanza*. Have you ever seen *Bonanza*, with Ben Cartwright, Adam, Hoss, and Little Joe? Do you remember those characters and that show?

Bonanza presents the perfect picture of our covenant. The show took place in the Nevada Territory in the Wild West days. The Cartwrights owned a very large, fenced-in ranch called the Ponderosa. The choicest piece of property in the entire territory, the Ponderosa was located near Lake Tahoe and actually had fresh water running through it.

If you lived on the Ponderosa, life was really good. Hoss didn't miss too many meals. You reckon they had provisions? Oh yeah, they had plenty laid in store. And they had prosperity. They had lots of cattle, the best cattle in the land. They had the best fields, with green grass, because they had water. And mean and greedy folks would try to take the cattle, the water, and even the Ponderosa land, and the Cartwrights would have to go out and defend the boundaries of their ranch.

You know what else they had on the Ponderosa? They had some fine horses. Now, Little Joe and Hoss, they didn't ride some old, broken-down mules. They had nice paints and ponies and pintos. Yes sir, they had some fine horses. They had the best rides of the day. And did you notice that every time one of the men got hurt or shot, after they got back to the Ponderosa, they always healed up, every time, no matter how sick they were? They would go out on the trail and get shot or sick. What would they do? They would take their sick and wounded back to the Ponderosa, and once they were inside the boundaries, inside that great big house, with all the Pottery Barn furniture, they would heal up, usually within an hour, unless it was a two-part episode. The life on the Ponderosa is a picture of God's covenant with us. When He says, "Obey My commandments" or "Observe to do My Word," He is just setting out a fence line for us. And if you live on God's Ponderosa, your life can literally be heaven on earth.

I know you're sitting there thinking: *That's pie in the sky, Andrew. What you say is really nice in theory, but you don't know what I'm going through.* You are correct; I don't know what you're going through. And heaven on earth does sound like a nice theory, but I didn't think of it myself. Who cares what I say, anyway? Let's see what the Bible says about it and what Jesus said about it. Everybody reading this book, I guarantee you that, what I'm about to quote to you, you could quote right back with me.

Here is what Jesus says about having heaven on earth.

Our father, which art in heaven, Hallowed be thy name. Thy kingdom come. Thy will be done on earth as it is in Heaven.

Matthew 6:9

HOLD THE PHONE! "On earth as it is in heaven" – "Thy will be done"? Are you kidding me?

When somebody dies, he leaves a last will and....what? Testament. Oh, right: his last will and testament. We have the New Testament and Old Testament, new covenant and old covenant.

So really we could say: "Thy covenant be done on earth as it is in heaven."

Some of you will argue that the wording is a stretch. All right: let's just stick with the word "will." In heaven, do you think that, after about a thousand years of living in that big mansion Jesus built for you, some angel in a cheap suit will show up on the doorstep with foreclosure papers? Does heaven have bankruptcy court? Really? What about a repo man? Do you think someone would repossess your car in heaven? Somebody just thought: *We won't have cars in heaven.* But you know we will all have a house. You know nobody is going to foreclose on your mansion in heaven.

In the New Jerusalem, do you think that Peter and Paul run a downtown soup kitchen or mission to feed the homeless and the hungry people? No. So God's will is not for you to be hungry or homeless. What about cancer? That disease affects pretty much everybody in some way or another. Do you think that St. Luke's Hospital in New Jerusalem has an oncologist? In heaven, will you have to go over to the hospice or schedule chemotherapy treatment? That's not God's will, is it? Of course, not! In heaven, He says that He'll wipe away every tear and that He'll destroy all sickness, disease, and suffering.

All right, so we know God's will in heaven, and Jesus said we could have His will on earth, as it is in heaven. What does He mean? He's talking about living a covenant-filled life, the kind that's available to everybody who will live inside the boundaries of God's Ponderosa here on earth. He's not trying to take away your fun. He's trying to show you the freedom and, yes, the fun you will have if you live inside the boundaries of the covenant. So don't think of the Bible and your relationship with God as a list of **DO's** and **DON'Ts**.

Definition of a Covenant

Before we go any further, let's look at the legal definition of covenant. According to Legal-Explanations. com, a covenant is "A LEGALLY BINDING CONTRACT; A COMPACT OR AGREEMENT UNDER

SEAL, MORE THAN A CONTRACT -ITS VALIDITY
IS AUTOMATIC IN A COURT OF EQUITY."

A covenant is more binding than a contract, and it cannot be disputed in court. The fine print doesn't matter, because no secret loophole or way out exists. Once you enter into a covenant, it's a done deal: period, end of story, game, set, and match. No judge can rule against the agreement or cause it to be null and void. Wow! That's more than a contract!

Where did the Covenant start?

Let's all get into a time machine and go back in time, all the way back to the beginning, before creation started. I realize I'm talking pretty far back here, but I'm setting us up for *Covenant for Rookies*. We need to lay a foundation before we get to those three words that sum up the entire covenant. Remember those three words? We'll get to them soon, I promise.

The LORD by wisdom hath founded the earth; by understanding hath he established the heavens.

Proverbs 3:16

The Lord by wisdom (remember wisdom, it'll come up again) founded the earth. "Founded" is a construction term. In construction, laying the foundation comes at the very beginning of the project. So by wisdom, God started the big real estate development project known as "the earth". That statement appears in the Old Testament, the old covenant; now let's look over in the New Testament, the new covenant, and see the similarities.

Through faith we understand that the worlds were framed by the word of God, so that things which are seen were not made of things which do appear.

Hebrews 11:3

Through faith we understand that the Word of God framed the worlds. "Framed" is also a construction term. God laid the foundation of the world, and now He's framing it, and not just planet earth. The Word of God framed all the planets. Now that's a real estate development project! Golf on Saturn? Condos with a star-front view of the Milky Way, anyone?

In these two places, we see two different terms: "wisdom" and "the Word of God". Both terms describe doing exactly the same things: building, creating, constructing. Wisdom is the Word of God, and the Word of God is wisdom: they are the same. But let everything be established by two or three witnesses. Let's keep going, and we'll see another set of Scriptures proving the point.

We're going to go back to wisdom first. In Proverbs 8, I'm going to start in verse 12 and jump to 22; we'll read all the in-between verses eventually. This passage is like a Shakespeare play, when Macbeth does his soliloquy, or like a talk radio show, when the host does his monologue. Wisdom is doing a monologue, and it starts in verse 12.

I wisdom dwell with prudence, and find out knowledge of witty inventions...The LORD possessed me in the beginning of his way, before his works of old. I was set up from everlasting, from the beginning, or ever the earth was. When there were no depths, I was brought forth; when there were no fountains abounding with water. Before the mountains were settled, before the hills was I brought forth: while as yet he had not made the earth, nor the fields, nor the highest part of the dust of the world. When he prepared the heavens, I was there: when he set a compass upon the face of the depth: when he established the clouds above: when he strengthened the fountains of the deep: when he gave to the sea his decree, that the waters should not pass his commandment: when he appointed the foundations of the earth: Then I was by him, as one brought up with him: and I was daily his delight, rejoicing always before

him; rejoicing in the habitable part of his earth; and my delights were with the sons of men.

Proverbs 8:12; 22-31

There is wisdom, one with God, from the beginning, from everlasting, before the earth ever was. Wisdom testifies to the process of how God made the planet, and not just eyewitness testimony, but the expert testimony of a participant. Remember Proverbs 3:19; wisdom founded the earth.

How does what we just read line up with what we've said about the Word of God being the same as wisdom? I'm glad you asked.

In the beginning was the Word, and the Word was with God, and the Word was God. The same was in the beginning with God. All things were made by him; and without him was not any thing made that was made.

John 1:1-3

Looking at all these passages of Scripture, we can see that wisdom and the Word of God truly are the same. They both did the exact same things during creation. The same language and terminology describes their traits and attributes. They were both there in the beginning. They were both one with God. They were with God, and they made everything. Whenever you see "wisdom", it's synonymous with "the Word of God", and the Word of God is our covenant. The Old Testament (covenant) and the New Testament (covenant) together make up our covenant. Do you see the connection, that wisdom is the Word of God?

We can have wisdom, or be wise, by "doing the Word", or "observing to do all the commandments", or "hearkening diligently to the voice of the Lord", or "obeying all that He commands". Every time you see these phrases in the Bible, God is spurring us on to be wise. Being wise, or acting in wisdom, is simply living on God's Ponderosa. Whenever you see the terms "obey God", or "do His commandments", or "do the Word", "be a doer, not just a hearer", "hearken diligently", a red flag should go off in your mind as a reminder to live inside the boundaries of the covenant. Our covenant is not a checklist of do's and don'ts. It's just living inside the fence line of God's Ponderosa.

Wisdom is the Covenant

The reason that I showed you that wisdom is the same as the Word is because *Covenant for Rookies* (those three words) comes from wisdom. Wisdom brings with it many advantages, and if you get wisdom (the Word of God) then you are getting the covenant and all the benefits of the covenant.

Get wisdom, get understanding: forget it not; neither decline from the words of my mouth. Forsake her not, and she shall preserve thee: love her, and she shall keep thee. Wisdom is the principal thing; therefore get wisdom: and with all thy getting get understanding.

Proverbs 4-5-7

What's the principal thing, the first, most important element? Wisdom. Wisdom is the main object, the number one priority. Or we could put it this way: the Word of God is the main thing, the number one thing. Nobody who is born again can argue with that statement. The Word of God is the main thing. This Scripture says to you, whatever you do, get wisdom, because when you get wisdom, when you go after the Word, when you live on God's Ponderosa, that's when you get all the benefits of the covenant.

Happy is the man that findeth wisdom, and the man that getteth understanding. For the merchandise of it is better than the merchandise of silver, and the gain thereof than fine gold. She is more precious than rubies: and all the things thou canst desire are not to be compared unto her. Length of days is in her right hand; and in her left hand riches and honour.

Proverbs 3:13-16

Did you notice what wisdom is holding in her hands? If you go after wisdom (the Word), and you get wisdom (the Word), you also get what's in her hands.

Getting Wisdom: The Magic Formula

Buckle up! I know that we are flying through a lot Scripture, but we should want to know what the Word says. Who cares what I think? The Word of God is a legal document, and if we can see with our own eyes what legally belongs to us, claiming it is much easier. God can't legally get the benefits of the covenant to you unless you follow the rules and laws that govern covenants. God won't do anything illegal; He's not a criminal.

He sent redemption unto his people: he hath commanded his Covenant forever: holy and reverend is his name. The fear of the LORD is the beginning of wisdom: a good understanding have all they

that do his commandments: his praise endureth forever.

Psalm 111:9-10

We know that when we get wisdom, we get the benefits of the covenant. *Great, thanks for telling us what we need, Andrew.* Simply telling you what you need without telling you how to get it is wrong. Plenty of people love to tell you what you need to do, but most of them are short on the "how to do it" part. I'm not one of those folks. The question is: How do we get wisdom so that we can get all the benefits of the covenant? God is so good that He breaks the answer down into a simple formula or equation. Psalm 111:10 gives us the first part of the equation for getting wisdom. The beginning of wisdom, the first step in getting wisdom, is "**the fear of the Lord**".

I want to show you this part of the equation again. This Scripture in Psalms is not just one single reference in the middle of nowhere.

The fear of the LORD is the beginning of wisdom: and the knowledge of the holy is understanding.

Proverbs 9:10

The jumping off point, the launching pad to get wisdom is **"the fear of the Lord"**. Well what does that phrase mean? What is "the fear of the Lord"? Don't panic; I've done all the heavy lifting for you on this one. I informally surveyed quite a number of folks, conducting what you might call "man on the street" interviews. All the answers folks gave me boil down to two responses.

Most people said that "the fear of the Lord" is reverential respect. That's a pretty good answer. But I know some fools, I mean fools now, that won't cuss around the preacher, and when they do they say, "I'm sorry," because they have reverential respect for God: not for the preacher, but for God. But they're still fools. They don't have wisdom; anyone who looks at what their lives are like can tell they don't have wisdom. So, is reverential respect the beginning of wisdom? No.

The other answer I received was that "the fear of the Lord" is when you're afraid of God. "When you're doing wrong, He'll strike you down." I know a large number of ministers whose slogan is, "Put the fear of God in them". That's the beginning of wisdom? No. **James 2:19** says that the demons believe, and they tremble. They're afraid of God, very afraid. The demons and all the devils of hell, are they wise? Do they have wisdom? No, they are all fools. The original fool is Lucifer.

We know what "the fear of the Lord" isn't. Now let's find out what "the fear of the Lord" is.

The fear of the LORD is to hate evil: pride, and arrogancy, and the evil way, and the froward mouth, do I hate.

Proverbs 8:13

The "fear of the Lord" is to hate? HATE? Yes, HATE! I realize that our mamas all taught us not to hate, but I didn't say so. God did. You can argue with Him about it. The word "hate" in the original Hebrew literally means, "to make a personal enemy of". This verse spells out exactly what "the fear of the Lord" is; it is to HATE four things. We must make a personal enemy of evil, pride and arrogancy, the evil way, and the froward mouth. In order to "fear the Lord", you must hate each of those things; hate, not disdain, not dislike, not tolerate, but HATE and want to kill those things, because if you don't, they will kill you.

Let's start with "evil". It is not what we think it is. Society, television, movies, pop culture, and especially Christian media have twisted the true meaning of evil. When we think of the word "evil", we think of things like murdering, cheating, lying, illicit sex, stealing, and killing. Evil is not any of those things. Those things are works of the flesh, iniquities, trespasses, and transgressions, not evil.

And then we think that unrighteousness is evil. No, whenever you see the word "righteous" or "unrighteous", it is talking about who has equity with God or who doesn't have equity with God. Righteousness designates who is in the covenant, and unrighteousness designates who isn't in the covenant. The righteous person is in God's family, while the unrighteous person is not. So unrigh-teousness is not evil. So what is evil?

The Hebrew word for evil is the word *ra-ah* (pro-nounced "raw-aw") and it is a word that possesses fifteen attributes. Ra-ah is actually a list of fifteen categories, each one being "evil". (Remember, we are to hate, make a personal enemy of each of these fifteen things.) Here's the list. Have any of these ever showed up in your life? If you want to **fear the Lord**, then you have to HATE each of the things on this list.

Adversity. Affliction. Calamity. Displeasure. Distress **(WORRY)**. Exceeding great grief. Harm. Heaviness. Hurt. Ill favor (when somebody doesn't like you). Misery. Sadness. Sorrow. Trouble. Wrong.

(For an in-depth study on the true meanings of good and evil, go to www.thecloc.com; "Audio Archives" and click on the MP3 files "Back to Basics: Good and Evil".)

That list of woes is the true meaning of evil. Evil is anything that's outside of our covenant, and our covenant is the Word of God, which is the same as wisdom. And the beginning of wisdom is "the fear of the Lord", which is to hate all the stuff that's not in our covenant. Evil is being unable to pay your bills. Evil is being sick, whether it's a cold or cancer. Evil is having unharmonious relationships with your spouse, your kids, your family members, and your boss, folks at work, your neighbors, or whoever else is giving you a hard time. Those things are evil. God says that to hate evil is the beginning of wisdom. When you hate that garbage like a personal enemy, when you hate being sick, when you hate financial lack, when you hate trouble, when you hate depression, when you hate being anxious: when you get to the point in life that you hate everything on that list, then you're onto the beginning of wisdom.

The second thing to hate is pride and arrogancy. This statement is self-explanatory, but we will discuss it at greater depth a little later.

That brings us to hating the "evil way". We know that evil is that list of fifteen; well, the word "way" in the Hebrew literally means a course of life, a manner of life, or a life-style. We need to make a personal enemy of an entire manner of life, or a life-style of adversity, affliction, calamity, displeasure, anxiety, misery, etc. Do you know anybody whose entire life is misery? Do you know anybody who is just plain miserable all the time? That life is the "evil way". What about anxiety, worry, or depression? What about affliction? Do you know anybody who is constantly plagued by some ache, pain, or sickness? Plug in any word from the list of "evil" and test yourself. Are you hating the evil way or living the evil way? If you've been living there, don't fret; only "fear the Lord" and begin to hate living like that. Make walking in evil your personal enemy! Doing so is the beginning of wisdom, step number one of enjoying your covenant.

Finally, hate the "froward mouth". What is that? Froward means "to overturn" and mouth means speech. You must hate to overturn what God says about you with your own speech. You must make a personal enemy of your mouth when words that contradict the Word of God come out of it. The study of this principal alone would fill an entire book. *(To get more in-depth teaching on this topic, go to www.thecloc.com audio archives page and listen to "Done Deal" parts 1 and 2.)* Suffice it to say, if you can't say what God says about you, then you should just zip your lips!

We are learning quite a bit. We now know that "the fear of the Lord" is to hate evil, pride and arrogancy, the evil way, and the froward mouth. The equation for wisdom is beginning to take shape.

Wisdom = the fear of the Lord + humility

The final factor in the formula also appears in Proverbs.

By humility and the fear of the LORD are riches, and honour, and life.

Proverbs 22:4

The final factor to the equation of wisdom is humility. Religious thinking has twisted what this word means. Religion teaches us that, if we are humble, we should think and act like this: "Oh, I'm just a worm in the dirt for Jesus. I'm not proud. My family is just barely making it, but we're just going to tough it out until we get heaven. I'm just being humble." That kind of self-abuse is NOT humility. The true meaning of humility is believing, actually believing, that God is smarter than you are. Do you think that God is at least as smart as you are? Authentic humility is acting like He is smarter than you.

Do you remember Moses and the children of Israel? You've seen the movie *The Ten Commandments* with Charlton Heston, haven't you? The Hebrew slaves finally escape from Egypt after the ten plagues. They are camped by the Red Sea, with mountains on each side, and then the most heavily armed military force in the world comes after them to kill them. What are they going do? God tells Moses, "Take that stick that is in your hand, that dead tree branch, and hold it out over the ocean, and I'll make a way for you to escape."

Now, Moses was brought up in Pharaoh's house, because Pharaoh's daughter had adopted him. He went to the finest universities and had the finest education, including military and political training. He was in on the architecture and building of the pyramids. He was a smart guy, one of the smartest guys on the planet, and he was being groomed to take over as the Pharaoh of Egypt. He knew the laws of physics of his day; he knew that holding a stick out over the ocean was not going to do anything. What was Moses' response to God? "God? I mean, come on. You know, I've got a BS and my master's in engineering from Cairo University. And You know I've got my PhD, as well. And we both know that it's pointless and ludicrous to hold my rod over the sea."

But do you know what? He believed that God knew what He was doing, and so he acted like God knew what He was doing, even if he didn't really believe it. He acted like God was smarter than he was, and he held that stick out over the

Red Sea. And the waters parted so that the people could walk through, and they won.

The Hebrew nation would have died right then and there had Moses not believed and acted like God was smarter. That is a picture of humility. Humility is not some religious "I'm just humble, I'm just meek, I'll just turn the other cheek," philosophy. Simply believe and act like God's smarter than you, and you've got this humility thing licked!

Let's go back to **Proverbs 22:4**, because in this verse are those three words. (Remember the three words?) This verse is *Covenant for Rookies.* Write this verse down on a bunch of sticky notes and plaster them all over your mirrors, the refrigerator, the dashboard of your vehicle, etc. If you want to know what your covenant is, this is it right here. **Proverbs 22:4 is *Covenant for Rookies*.** If you don't remember any other verse in the Bible, remember this one, because this is your covenant, and it's boiled down in plain English, for regular folk, so that it's easy to remember. God boiled it down on purpose for you to get it. When you are in the thick of things, in the heat of battle, under the crush, and life is kicking you in the teeth, you don't have time to go through this big, giant legal document (the Bible), to figure out what is part of the covenant and what isn't. You need to know, on the fly, in real life and in real time, what to grab onto, what your legal standing is. Buckle up, because here it is, those three words. *Covenant for Rookies*: "**By humility and the fear of the LORD are riches, and honour, and life.**"

<u>RICHES, HONOR, and LIFE</u>

Those three words are the entire covenant. Everything that God has for you, every benefit of the covenant, every promise He has made, falls into one of those three categories: (1) riches, (2) honor, or (3) life.

But how do you get it? If you believe God's smarter than you and act like it (humility), and you hate evil, adversity, affliction, misery, worry, lack, poverty, sickness, bad relationships, shame, and all that is garbage in life, making them your personal enemy (the fear of the Lord), then you get wisdom, and wisdom brings to you riches, honor, and life. *Covenant for Rookies* is **riches and honor and life**. Say it out loud, "My covenant with God is riches, honor and life. If it's riches, honor, and life, it's part of my covenant, and it's from God. If it's not riches, honor, and life, it's NOT part of my covenant, and it's NOT from God. So dump it!"

Notice in Proverbs 3:16 that wisdom is holding three things: length of days (LIFE) is in one hand, and in the other hand is RICHES and HONOR. Wisdom = Riches, Honor, and Life. And humility + the fear of the Lord = Riches, Honor, and Life. Therefore, humility + the fear of the Lord = Wisdom. Those equations are the formula for the covenant.

Let's explore what each one of them means. **Riches**: the King James Version translated it "riches", but the Hebrew word means exactly **wealth far richer than riches**. We'll talk about that definition in a minute, because that one gets some folks really upset. **Honor** means privilege, rank, and title. If you have honor, you're a privileged person of rank and title. And **life** means you have a long, healthy, high-quality time here on earth that just continues forever.

LIFE

All right, let's discuss **life** first, because that's the easiest one for us to swallow. We'll start here, because when you say riches in church, people immediately think, "Mm-Hmm, watch it preacher; money is the root of all evil." No, the **love** of money is the root of all evil. It's okay. We'll talk about riches later. We'll start with life.

My son, forget not my law; but let thine heart keep my commandments: for length of days, and long life, and peace, shall they add to thee. Let not mercy and truth forsake thee: bind them about thy neck; write them on the table of thine heart: so shalt thou find favor and good success in the sight of God and man. Her ways are ways of pleasantness, and all her paths are peace. She is a tree of life

to them that lay hold on her: and <u>happy</u> is everyone that retaineth her.

Proverbs 3:1-4, 17-18

(emphasis mine)

Please notice the underlined words in the verses above: length of days, long life, and peace (verse 2); favor and good success (or good understanding) (verse 4); pleasantness and peace (verse 17); tree of life and happy (verse 18).

Here is how the Bible, your covenant, defines life. Life encompasses all of the underlined words above, including health. You get to be healthy. You don't have to be healthy, but good health is part of the covenant. If you aren't healthy, you definitely won't have length of days or long life. You don't even have to have the sniffles or allergies, but whether you want to or not is up to you. (Remember the Ponderosa, the fence line, and living within the borders of the covenant). Good health doesn't just fall on you. Then, consider happiness. You get happiness. Proverbs says happy is the man..."**Happy.**"

When you're happy, you're having a good time. Life doesn't stink when you live inside the covenant.

The next thing is harmonious relationships. When you're pleasant, when you have pleasantness or peace, you have harmonious relationships with your spouse, with your kids, with your siblings, with your mama and daddy, with your neighbors, with your boss, and with your coworkers; you get to have harmonious relationships with all of them. That kind of harmony is covenant life. Life in the covenant is a long, healthy, high-quality life, filled with good relationships. And the icing on the cake (you know, the one you get to have and eat too) is happiness.

Just the **life** component of the covenant is off the hook! But it gets better, and there is so much more!

HONOR

Let's discover how the covenant defines **honor**. We're going back to Proverbs 8, right back into the middle of that monologue, and starting in verse 14. Remember who's doing the talking? Wisdom is talking.

> **Counsel is mine, and sound wisdom: I am understanding; I have strength. By me <u>kings</u> reign, and <u>princes</u> decree justice. By me <u>princes</u> rule, and <u>nobles</u>, even all the <u>judges</u> of the earth.**
>
> **Proverbs 8:14-16**
>
> **(emphasis mine)**

I underlined kings, princes, nobles, and judges. All those folks have honor. They're in positions of honor. They each have privilege and rank and title. Now, some folks in religious circles would never say they want to be in a position of honor, because that desire wouldn't be humble: "I'm just trying to be humble and have humility." Those folks are giving a good "church answer", but they're lying. God enjoys being honored, and He created us in His image. We're just like Him; so we also enjoy being honored. This quality is part of your covenant; you should be in a position of honor.

After reading this passage, I thought, "I can't be a king! I'm an American. We don't have kings. President is possible, but not a king." In this world, not too many folks will be either king, president, or head of state. We simply don't have that many nations. So I can effectively scratch that job title off the list for almost everybody.

Next comes being a prince or princess, and being an American, I'm not of royal blood. Most people of the world are not of royal blood; so that cuts that job off the list as well as king, which brings up being a judge. Unless I do a complete career change and go to law school, pass the bar exam, and get the political hook-up to score an appointment to the bench, I've got no shot at a judgeship. Most of the people of the covenant are not going to be judges, either (although you do have a better chance of becoming a judge then a king or prince).

That leaves being a noble. What is a noble? It sounds very King Arthur and Camelot. Exactly! A noble is a person of privilege, rank, title, and heredity. And since you entered the covenant, you became part of God's family, and so you now have heredity with Him. So, each and every one of us has a shot at being a noble. Noblemen in old England (King Arthur and Camelot times) were just a bunch of people who happened to own a lot of land. Those large tracts of land produced lots of income via the peasants who lived on the land and paid lots and lots of rent to the landlords or nobles. That's all the nobles were, rich people, and because of inheriting those riches, they got the title, the rank, and the privilege. All it took was money to become a noble and be in a position of honor.

RICHES

This history lesson brings us squarely to the first part of the covenant, RICHES! Let's continue reading Wisdom's monologue.

I love them that love me; and those that seek me early shall find me. Riches and

honor are with me; yea, <u>durable riches</u> and righteousness.

Proverbs 8:17-18

(emphasis mine)

I hear most Christians say that "I'm just rich in family" or "I'm rich in love. That's really what God was talking about." **No!** Did you read the underlined words? The Bible says **"durable riches"**!

When the government comes out with the gross domestic product or the gross national product and all the quarterly economic stats, they have one category called "services." The plumber and the HVAC guy coming to your house, or the delivery driver, etc., are in the services category. But there's another category, and that category is called "goods." And under goods we find consumables, which are food and drugs, as well as what's called "durable goods." Durable goods are things that last, that you can put your hands on. Your car is a durable good. Your house is a durable good. Your refrigerators, your washing machines, your computers, and your TVs are all durable goods.

These items are all called durable goods, because they last and you can put your hands on them. Wisdom uses this same word to describe and define covenant riches, **durable riches,** which are physical riches, the kind you can put your hands on and spend. Let's continue with the monologue:

> **My fruit is better than gold, yea, than fine gold; and my <u>revenue</u>, than choice silver.**
>
> **Proverbs 8:19**
>
> **(emphasis mine)**

Again, notice the underlined word, revenue. In the Hebrew, this word actually means income or paycheck. So when you hook up with wisdom (covenant), the paycheck of wisdom (covenant) is **better** than fine gold and choice silver.

Somebody just said, "See, the riches in the Bible are better than silver and gold."

Yeah, that's right. Let's ask the question: What is better than silver or gold? If we asked, say, Bill Gates what was better than silver or gold, he could tell us about how he made 0s and 1s into much better than silver or gold. (That's what he did with binary code; he wrote a bunch of 0s and 1s and pumped out $65 billion worth of Microsoft products). How are those 0s and 1s better? Where would he store $65 billion of silver or gold? Do you know how much that would weigh?

What's worth more than gold? Ask Intel if they'd trade their silicone for gold. You can't make processor chips out of gold. Who knew sand would be better than gold? Wisdom did, because wisdom founded the earth, and sand and gold are part of the earth.

So what's better than gold? Well, lots of stuff is better than gold. We've already said sand and silicon and 0s and 1s, and then we have to count oil and natural gas that are way better than gold. So you don't have to wait for the buried treasure to fall on your head. Wisdom (covenant) has a paycheck, and whatever it is (God will give you ideas) is better than gold or silver. If you look back in verse 12, the beginning of the monologue, Wisdom says, **"I wisdom dwell with prudence, and I find out knowledge of witty inventions."** Living inside the covenant produces knowledge of witty inventions, and witty inventions produce riches. Whenever I read that verse, I always think of the clapper. Do you remember the clapper? That's a witty invention. That guy's rich. Who knew the clapper would be better than gold, for crying out loud?

Continuing with Wisdom's monologue:

I lead in the way of righteousness, in the midst of the paths of judgment; that I may cause those that love me to inherit <u>substance</u>; and I will fill their <u>treasures</u>.

Proverbs 8:20-21

(emphasis mine)

Substance: that's physical stuff in this life you can put your hands on. Then Wisdom says, "And I will fill their treasures." In the Hebrew, the exact word that is translated "treasures" in the King James is **depository**. Wisdom literally says, "I will fill your depositories".

I don't know about you, but my depository is my checking account. My checking account has never been so full that the bank called me up and told me, "Hey, look, it is full to the max. You're going to have to open another account somewhere else, because your account is too full." So I'm not there yet, but this covenant says that your depository will be filled. Whether it's your 401k, whether it's your money market, whether it's your CDs, whatever your choice of financial instrument is, wherever you put your money, wherever you make your deposits, God says they will be filled when you get wisdom. When you hook up with wisdom and the covenant, then you get your depository filled.

I stated earlier that the Hebrew meaning for riches was literally wealth far richer than riches. Well, what did I mean? I watch that show *The Apprentice* with Donald Trump. I like to watch that show. Donald Trump: now here's a guy who has got riches. He's got the helicopter. He's got the jets. He's got the big penthouse. He's got the yacht. So he's got riches. Well, what is wealth far greater than riches? Donald Trump has riches, and God promises you wealth far greater than what Trump has. That promise blows my mind; I can hardly get my head or my mind around it. But until you can believe it, you'll never receive it. Mark 11:24 says that you only receive if you believe first. If you don't really believe, then you won't really receive.

Therefore I say unto you, What things soever ye desire, when ye pray, believe that ye receive them, and ye shall have them.

Mark 11:24

Here's the agreement: when we live inside God's Ponderosa (which just means believing that He's smarter than we are and hating anything that's not riches, honor and life), and we do the Word (make decisions based on the Bible), we get wisdom. Remember, wisdom is the principle thing. Wisdom for us is the Word of God in action in our life. It's just simply doing the Word. I repeat: Wisdom is doing the Word. What does "doing the Word" mean? Whatever Bible you know, you just start to make decisions in your life based on what you know. When you do so, then He'll give you more information, and you'll begin to grow in your covenant.

You grow from faith (one level of believing) to faith (to the next level of believing). You just don't land in a pile of money, boom, and now you have riches far greater than wealth, or wealth greater than Donald Trump. Bill Gates didn't start off with $65 billion, either. He had a garage and an idea. The key to how much riches, honor, and life you enjoy depends on how much you can believe and how many decisions you make based on the Wisdom of the Word of God.

Let's look at what Jesus says. Don't take this personally, but I don't care what the experts think, or what you think, or even what I think. I want to know what God thinks and adopt that thinking. So if something is in the Bible, I must adjust my thinking or my opinions to what the Word of God says. Most people, when confronted with the truth that God wants you to have riches, honor, and life, tell me, "Well, I just don't believe it like that. Why would God want to do that for me?" You most likely know this story Jesus tells. This story is, in a nutshell, how to get the riches, honor, and life which come from wisdom or being wise.

> **Therefore whosoever heareth these sayings of mine, and doeth them, I will liken him unto a wise man, which built his house upon a rock: and the rain descended, and the floods came, and the winds blew, and beat upon that house; and it fell not: for it was founded upon a rock. And every one that heareth these sayings of mine, and doeth them not, shall be likened unto a foolish man, which built his house upon the sand: and the rain descended, and the floods came, and the winds blew, and beat upon that house; and it fell: and great was the fall of it.**
>
> **Matthew 7:24-27**

Whosoever hears the sayings of Jesus and does them is a wise man, someone who has wisdom, and wisdom brings riches, honor, and life. So when you hear the Word and you do it, you get wisdom; so you are building your life on a solid foundation. When all the junk, all the evil comes, all the adversity, all the affliction, and all that is **not** riches, honor, and life, nothing happens. Because you did the Word and you got wisdom, your life is not shaken, and you win. That's the covenant. You do the Word, and you win.

Conversely, everyone that hears the sayings of Jesus and does not do them is a fool, someone who ignores the wisdom of the Word when making decisions. The person who hears the Word and doesn't do it has no wisdom, and he is building his life on shifting sand that has no foundation. When all the junk, all the evil comes, all the adversity, all the affliction, and all that is **not** riches, honor, and life, he crashes and burns. Because he did not do the Word, he has no wisdom.

These two guys were neighbors. They lived right next door to each other. They both went to the same church. They went to hear Jesus teach, because they both heard Jesus' words. They both probably said, "Hallelujah, Amen," at the same time. They both probably gave in the offering. They both maybe plugged in to the Temple. One of them did Sunday school, and one of them worked in the nursery. But what was the difference between them? One did the Word, and one didn't.

When you do the Word, when you live inside the boundaries of the covenant and you live on God's Ponderosa, then Jesus said you're a wise man. What does wisdom bring us? Wisdom brings riches, honor, and life. So the extent to which you do the Word is the extent to which you're going to experience riches, honor, and life. Your quality of life has nothing to do with being "saved". The two people in Jesus' illustration were both covenant people, both going to the same church, both listening to the same message. They probably carpooled to meetings and listened to the same CDs and tapes. However, one of them had victory, riches, honor, and life, while the other one didn't. Riches, honor, and life are not going to fall on you automatically. If you don't live in the covenant, you won't experience its benefits.

A Covenant-filled Life

Before we go into all of the details of the covenant, I want to discuss what life inside the boundaries of the covenant looks like.

Because we will be reading out of the Old Testament, some people will say, "Well, that was for the Hebrews and the Israelites; it doesn't pertain to us." So what I want to do is show you in the Bible, in the New Testament, the new covenant, that it does pertain to us. God entered into covenant with Abraham. Abraham is called the father of our faith. The covenant started with him, and we will study that beginning in greater depth a little later. But we are proving that benefits of the covenant listed in the Old Testament pertain to us, right now, today.

> **Even as Abraham believed God, and it was accounted to him for righteousness. Know ye therefore that they which are of faith, the same are the children of Abraham.**
>
> **Galatians 3:6-7**

If you are of faith, if you have accepted Jesus, then you are considered one of the children of Abraham.

So then they which be of faith are blessed with faithful Abraham.

Galatians 3:9

Again, if you are a person of faith, if you believe in Jesus, you are blessed (have the same blessings) with Abraham.

Christ hath redeemed us from the curse of the law, being made a curse for us: for it is written, Cursed is every one that hangeth on a tree: that the blessing of Abraham might come on the Gentiles through Jesus Christ; that we might receive the promise of the Spirit through faith.

Galatians 3:13-14

This passage very clearly states that, no matter what your physical, natural ancestry is, if you have been born again (received Jesus as your Lord and Savior), you are a descendant of Abraham and part of the covenant.

With our legal standing established, let's go back to the Old Testament and see exactly the blessing of Abraham that was also given to his descendants. Here is the covenant line: Abraham, Isaac and Jacob (whose name was also Israel), and the children of Israel are the physical descendants of the covenant that received Abraham's blessing. Until Jesus came, the blessing was only available to Israelites. It was not available to anybody else. But now, through Jesus' sacrifice, that blessing is available to anybody. What makes it a better covenant is that it's available to everybody.

Verse 14 uses the word "might." Did you notice that? Where it says, "That the blessing of Abraham **might** come on" you? Which also means it "**might not**" come on you. You can be born again and have faith in Jesus but not have all the blessings of Abraham show up in your life. They don't fall on you automatically. You have to do something first, and that something is to live inside the boundaries of the covenant (or God's Word). You don't have to obey a list of dos and don'ts, just simply live inside the boundaries of the covenant. Remember how we talked about living on God's Ponderosa?

I hear people say all the time, "Oh, it's so hard. I'm just trying to be a Christian." If you are born again, you are a Christian. If you believe on Jesus, you already are one; you don't have to try and be one. My son Jack isn't trying to be Jack. He is Jack. He was born Jack. When you get born again, you get God's nature put on the inside of you, and you are a Christian (little Christ). Being a Christian isn't really hard; if you are born again, you are a Christian. On the show *Bonanza*, did you ever hear Little Joe or Hoss or Adam say, "It's so hard living on the Ponderosa? I'm just trying to be a Cartwright." Have you ever seen them complaining about how hard it is living on the Ponderosa?

They still had to do work. They still had to deal with difficult situations in life. They still had to deal with difficult people, some trying to steal their stuff, some trying to hurt them, sometimes shooting at them (occasionally successfully). But all the hard things turned out for good in the end. If you would just hang in there for the entire hour episode, the hard places all ended up good. That's exactly how our covenant with God is; if you hang in there for the entire episode and don't stop the tape, don't change the channel, don't turn off the show during the commercial break, it ALWAYS turns out good, ALWAYS. If you live inside the boundaries of the covenant, everything will work out for your benefit. But if you jump over the back fence instead of staying inside the boundaries of the covenant, God can't help you. Someone just said, "Well, God's sovereign, and He can do what He wants." Let me ask you: Is the president of the United States sovereign in China? Of course not! We already know that a king is only sovereign in his own kingdom. God's kingdom, where He is sovereign, is inside the boundaries of covenant. When you jump the fence and go into another kingdom and stuff goes wrong, don't blame Him; you just entered the country where the blessing "might not" come on you.

Remember:

That the blessing of Abraham might come on the Gentiles through Jesus Christ; that we might receive the promise of the Spirit through faith.

Galatians 3:14

We get all the blessing through faith, by believing on Jesus. Let's look in the Old Testament at Deuteronomy, which actually means the second giving of the law. We're going to look at all the blessings of the law listed in the following passage.

And it shall come to pass, if thou shalt hearken diligently unto the voice of the LORD thy God, to observe *and* to do all his commandments which I command thee this day, that the LORD thy God will set thee on high above all nations of the earth.

Deuteronomy 28:1

Now, there's the catch. We only qualify to get all the blessings of Abraham because we believe on Jesus. But there's one more thing we have to do, and that is to observe and do all the commandments. So do we just have to keep the Ten Commandments? No, not at all, and we will discuss this point in great detail later on, after I lay the foundation for that discussion. But our sole requirement is simply living on the Ponderosa, living inside the boundaries of the covenant. It's not hard. It's not difficult. And God's not trying to steal your fun. But if you live inside the boundaries of the covenant, you get all these blessings.

And all these blessings shall come on thee, and overtake thee, if thou shalt hearken unto the voice of the LORD thy God.

Deuteronomy 28:2

The blessings will track you down and then tackle you, if you listen to the voice of the Lord your God. Twice now in two verses we notice specifically listening to God's voice: the spoken Word of

God, not the written Word of God. That distinction is a huge one. Romans 10:17 says that faith only comes from hearing the Word of God, but two different Greek words mean "word". The Greek word used in Romans 10:17 is *rhema,* which means spoken word, not *logos,* which means written word. Faith comes from hearing the spoken Word of God, His Spirit speaking directly to you. Here in Deuteronomy 28:1-2, we see that the blessings are contingent on our hearing and acting on God's voice, or His spoken Word. Keep that thought on the back burner on slow boil, and it will become clearer as we continue on.

We need to define the word "blessing" clearly, because we're going to see this word "blessing" quite a bit. If we researched the Hebrew, we'd find the word *barak,* which has two meanings, the literal meaning and then the cultural meaning. Literally, it means God kneeling down next to you and giving you a gift. Now, the Hebrews didn't know God as their father; they knew Him as their king. So, in a lot of people's minds, God would never kneel down and give them a gift. The word picture will make sense if you have ever seen someone kneel down to a child to give them something. If you're going give a small child a gift or you're going to help him tie his shoe, you kneel down to get on his level. That picture really shows what God's doing by kneeling down. When you see the word "blessed," it shows God kneeling down and getting on your level to give you help or give you a gift.

The second meaning of the word blessing, the cultural meaning, is consistently lucky success. When someone said that you were blessed, he meant that he recognized your consistent luck or consistent success. When I was brought up, my parents would say, "No, no, don't use the word 'lucky.' We're blessed." What the world sees when they see you having all the blessings of Abraham is what they know as luck. People talk about me this way constantly: "Man, that guy's lucky all the time. It's unbelievable how lucky that guy is." What the blessings of Abraham will do is show you to the outside world as that person who is lucky all the time. The word "blessed" basically means lucky. So when you read the verses below that say blessed or blessing, I want you to think in your mind consistently lucky or lucky all the time.

Blessed *shalt* thou *be* in the city, and blessed *shalt* thou *be* in the field.

Deuteronomy 28:3

Blessed, or consistently lucky, shalt thou be in the city. Now, we could just stop right there. He could've said just that one thing. You could've gone to Vegas or Monte Carlo and lived the rest of your life with the blessing of Abraham being consistently lucky in Vegas or Monte Carlo, and life would be good, wouldn't it? Wouldn't being consistently lucky in Vegas be a good thing for you? I mean, if you knew you would always win, playing the games wouldn't be gambling, because you would know you were going to win every time. So you could stop right there. But, no, those of us that didn't make it to Vegas or Monte Carlo, He says you're going to be blessed or consistently lucky in the field, or in the country, wherever you are. Whether you're in the city or the country, you're going to be consistently lucky.

> **Blessed *shall be* the fruit of thy body, and the fruit of thy ground, and the fruit of thy cattle, the increase of thy kine, and the flocks of thy sheep.**
>
> **Deuteronomy 28:4**

When this Scripture was written, the Hebrews had an agricultural economy, so you could just put in parentheses there your business. Whatever your business is, you're going to be blessed in it. You'll be consistently lucky. You'll have consistently lucky success. The blessing of Abraham means that your business will be successful.

> **Blessed *shall be* thy basket and thy store.**
>
> **Deuteronomy 28:5**

Today, our basket and our store are our refrigerator, our freezer, and our pantry. How does a refrigerator or a freezer get to be consistently lucky? Now, my freezer would consider itself lucky if it was filled with some filet mignon and some bacon-wrapped shrimp and a lot of moose tracks ice cream. Whatever your pantry needs, it'll be full. The blessing of Abraham means that you'll be full.

Blessed *shalt* thou *be* when thou comest in, and blessed *shalt* thou *be* when thou goest out.

Deuteronomy 28:6

You'll be lucky coming in and lucky going out. The promises just keep getting better, don't they? He could've stopped right there, but He didn't, because God's good all the time.

The LORD shall cause thine enemies that rise up against thee to be smitten before thy face: they shall come out against thee one way, and flee before thee seven ways.

Deuteronomy 28:7

The Lord will cause your enemies that rise up against you to be smitten before your face. They'll come out against you one way, and they'll flee from you seven ways, or flee from you in all directions.

We saw this promise on *Bonanza* all the time. If you notice, when the Cartwright's enemies would come up against them, they would usually ride up to the front gate of the Ponderosa. They'd be there in front of the house. But by the end of the show, they were going in all directions with the posse after them. But God will do exactly the same for you; when someone comes against you one way, He'll make them flee from you in seven different directions. That protection is the blessing of Abraham, and it's pretty lucky. So when troubles or trials come, remember this fact: you get to win, if you live inside the boundaries of the covenant. That's a covenant-filled life.

The LORD shall command the blessing upon thee in thy storehouses, and in all that thou settest thine hand unto; and

he shall bless thee in the land which the LORD thy God giveth thee.

Deuteronomy 28:8

The Lord shall command the blessing upon you and your storehouses. Storehouses were barns and grain silos, but now our storehouses are our checking account, our savings account, our money markets, our 401ks, and our IRAs. Now, what would make them consistently lucky? Man, for your mutual funds to keep going up would make them lucky, wouldn't it? Won't you be lucky if your IRA and your 401k keep doing well and your bank account's full? That's what he's talking about, and He didn't stop there. He says that whatever it is that you put your hand to will be successful, even if it's being a good mom or a good dad. Wouldn't this promise even apply to doing the landscaping in your yard? "Oh, that person has a green thumb." The blessing of a green thumb can come upon you if you live inside the Ponderosa. That promise sounds silly, but God loves you so much that you'll even do well in your landscaping. And Scripture says that He'll bless you in the land that the Lord your God gives you. Now, the Lord God gave me my land in Greer, SC; so I'm doing well here.

The LORD shall establish thee an holy people unto himself, as he hath sworn unto thee, if thou shalt keep the commandments of the LORD thy God, and walk in his ways.

Deuteronomy 28:9

The Lord shall establish you a holy people unto Himself, as He has sworn to you, if you keep the commandments of the Lord and walk in His ways. Now, what did He mean? Living on the Ponderosa, God's Ponderosa, is living inside the boundaries of the covenant.

And all people of the earth shall see that thou art called by the name of the LORD; and they shall be afraid of thee.

Deuteronomy 28:10

All the people of the earth shall see that you are called by the name of the Lord, and they'll be afraid or, as the actual translation says, they'll be in awe of you. They'll be afraid of you, but they'll be in awe. The same thing also happened on the Ponderosa all the time. Little Joe and Hoss would go into town, Virginia City, and if they got in trouble, they just said, "We're Ben Cartwright's boys." Then the other man would pause before he said: "You're a Cartwright?" The sons were called by the name of Cartwright, and people were in awe of them. Why? People did not feel awe because of what they did, but because of what their daddy did. They were just a couple of young boys. The same principle applies to you, except you are called by the name of the Lord. Your last name is God Almighty. He will cause people to say, "That's one of God's kids over there. Watch out. She's consistently lucky. She has success in whatever she does." Isn't reading the Bible fun?

And the LORD shall make thee plenteous in goods, in the fruit of thy body, and in

the fruit of thy cattle, and in the fruit of thy ground, in the land which the LORD sware unto thy fathers to give thee. The LORD shall open unto thee his good treasure, the heaven to give the rain unto thy land in his season, and to bless all the work of thine hand: and thou shalt lend unto many nations, and thou shalt not borrow. And the LORD shall make thee the head, and not the tail; and thou shalt be above only, and thou shalt not be beneath; if that thou hearken unto the commandments of the LORD thy God, which I command thee this day, to observe and to do *them.*

Deuteronomy 28:11-13

And the Lord shall open up unto thee His good treasure, the heaven to give rain unto thy land in its season and to bless all the work of thy hand, and thou shall lend to many nations and shall not borrow. And the Lord shall make thee the head and not the tail. One translation says that He'll make you the top dog. You'll always be on top. All of these consistently lucky successes come as a result of living inside the boundaries of the covenant, by making decisions based on the wisdom the Word. Receiving these blessings is not hard. A covenant-filled life is full of consistently lucky success or riches, honor, and life.

CHAPTER 2

The Covenant Ritual–
Where It All Began

Remember that a covenant is more than a contract. We need to find out why riches, honor, and life belong to us legally. This chapter is going to be kind of technical. I'll try not to make it boring, but understanding all the legalities of our covenant with God is important. We're going to go back to the beginning, where everything began.

Brethren, I speak after the manner of men; though it be but a man's covenant,

**yet if it be confirmed, no man disannul-
leth, or addeth thereto.**

Galatians 3:15

So we're talking about a man's covenant. What
we are going to see is that God will meet you wherever
you are. This relationship isn't just something He
imagined. He took man's invention of the covenant
and then came down to our level. Then Scripture
says that this relationship was confirmed.

**Now to Abraham and his seed were the
promises made. He saith not, And to
seeds, as of many; but as of one, And to
thy seed, which is Christ.**

Galatians 3:16

We have three players involved in the covenant.
God came down and cut covenant with Abraham
and his seed, which is Christ. Abraham, Christ,
and God are the three people that are involved in
the covenant-cutting ritual.

And this I say, that the covenant, that was confirmed before of God in Christ, the law, which was four hundred and thirty years after, cannot disannul, that it should make the promise of none effect.

Galatians 3:17

God confirmed man's covenant in Christ. We know from this verse that Christ was physically there, because the covenant was confirmed in Him. God is setting the scene of the covenant with Abraham, God the Father, and Christ the Son all present four hundred thirty years before God gave the law to Moses.

For if the inheritance be of the law, it is no more of promise: but God gave it to Abraham by promise.

Galatians 3:18

The law, which is also called the "old covenant", didn't come into being until Moses showed up, four hundred thirty years after God cut covenant with Abraham. So the law, the old covenant, was **NOT** part of God's original plan; it was a band-aid. It was a stop-gap measure that God was forced to put into place until He could complete the covenant through Jesus. The law was neither the first nor the best option. We'll study this truth in greater detail later on, but suffice it to say for now that God instituted the law to buy Himself some time on the planet, protecting the blood line of the covenant until He could get Jesus here to the earth, legally, as a man. The children of Israel had completely forgotten the covenant and ended up in slavery for four hundred years in Egypt. The law came to keep them inside the boundaries of the covenant (on God's Ponderosa, remember?) until Jesus was born. Even the law didn't keep them on track for long, but that's another bunch of stories.

Let's jump down to Galatians 3:26 and tie in the fact that the covenant legally belongs to us.

For ye are all the children of God by faith in Christ Jesus. For as many of you

as have been baptized into Christ have put on Christ. There is neither Jew nor Greek, there is neither bond nor free, there is neither male nor female: for ye are all one in Christ Jesus. And if ye be Christ's, then are ye Abraham's seed, and heirs according to the promise.

Galatians 3:26-29

Right here this passage says that we are one with Christ, but it goes even further. It calls us Abraham's seed, and in verse 16, who did it say was Abraham's seed? Christ. We just got called Christ. That passage just blows people's minds. When we are born of the Spirit or born again or baptized (the Greek word means immersed) into Christ, the Bible says that we are the body of Christ; when God looks at us, He sees Christ. Let me make the point with a silly example. If my friends Sam and Julia walked into church, I wouldn't see Sam's head on Julia's body or Julia's head with Sam's body. Sam's head is on Sam's body; Sam is one person, head and body together.

The same is true of Julia and you and me and Christ. If together we are the body of Christ and if Jesus is the head, aren't we one person? When we walk in to a room, God sees Christ. We're all one. We are Abraham's seed. We are legally adopted into the covenant when we put our faith in Jesus.

The First Covenant

To understand all of this "legally binding" stuff fully, we need to go all the way back to the beginning. The first time God makes a covenant with anybody is with Noah. Here's the short version of the timeline. God creates Adam and gives him the position of god of this world. Adam blows it. He commits high treason against God. Adam delivers the world to Satan when he eats the fruit salad Eve made for him from the tree of the knowledge of good and evil. God promises Adam and Eve that He will send them a redeemer and get the planet back into the hands of mankind. A thousand years goes by before anything happens except that mankind degenerates. With no law and no covenant, folks are going downhill fast, and the whole creation turns into a giant mess. Then Noah comes along, and God tells Noah to build the ark and to trust Him to save him and his family. And oh, by the way, the entire planet will be getting a wash and rinse job. When the flood waters abate, God makes the first covenant.

Looking at this first covenant, we don't really see any ritual or ceremony. God just shows up and makes a promise. Noah and God didn't go through any steps to establish the covenant. This scene takes place about a thousand years prior to God's covenant with Abraham.

And God spake unto Noah, and to his sons with him, saying, And I, behold, I establish my covenant with you, and with your seed after you; and with every living creature that is with you, of the fowl, of the cattle, and of every beast of the earth with you; from all that go out of the ark, to every beast of the earth. And I will establish my covenant with

you, neither shall all flesh be cut off any more by the waters of a flood; neither shall there any more be a flood to destroy the earth.

Genesis 9:8-11

God makes this first covenant with all of nature, not just with Noah, but Noah's son and their wives and their children to come thereafter, and all of the animals and all of the earth. Why did He do that?

God tells Noah and the earth and all of nature that He won't destroy it all again by water. God makes a covenant to seal the promise with "mother nature".

And God said, This is the token of the covenant which I make between me and you and every living creature that is with you, for perpetual generations: I do set my bow in the cloud, and it shall

be for a token of a covenant between me and the earth.

Genesis 9:12-13

This covenant is the very first ever recorded in the Bible. From the time Noah gets off the boat to the time that God meets Abraham, approximately a thousand years goes by.

Let's shoot ahead to a time between Noah and Abraham, in ancient times. Do you remember ever seeing those old *Hercules* and *Xena* shows on TV? The time of Nimrod is even before that time. Nimrod was an actual guy; the name is not just an insult you hurl at somebody for being a dip-dummy. The Bible says he was a mighty hunter that was against the Lord. He's the guy that started Babylon and the pagan god system. The entire culture and society of Babylon was based on paganism, worshipping the sun god, the moon god, etc. This culture came up with a ritual to seal an agreement or contract, which they called a covenant. The ritual was a nine-step process that evolved over time. By the time God met Abraham, the covenant process was widely recognized as the law of the land of that day. Remember that Galatians called it a man's covenant.

God didn't make up this ritual; it was invented by pagans. But God used the law of the land of that day to seal an agreement or contract with man, giving Him legal right to protect and to bless. What makes up this ritual? What are the nine steps? I'm glad you asked.

The Covenant Ritual – Nine Steps

The very first thing people did when they wanted to cut covenant with each other, a transaction which is, again, more than a legally binding contract, was to exchange coats with each other. The only thing to which I can relate this action in our modern culture is the letter jacket. Back in high school, when a girl was dating the quarterback, he would give that girl his varsity letterman's jacket, and she would wear his jacket, letting everyone know that she was going steady with Billy Bob, the star quarterback. That practice comes from this ritual, the exchange of coats with your partner in a covenant.

For the next step, the second step, the covenant candidates would exchange weapons. Weapons were personal and expensive, and they were usually family heirlooms. You couldn't go down to the Gun & Pawn and just pick out a new Glock 19. Weapons were hand crafted and custom made. The weapon exchange signified the candidates saying, "I'll fight your battles, and you will fight mine. Whatever fight one of us ends up in, when an enemy sees that we're holding each other's weapons, he'll realize that he'll have to fight two people now, not just one." That relationship is a major part of the covenant.

Step three of this ritual gets kind of gross, but it's a pagan ritual. The covenant candidates would take several animals and cut them down the center axis. They would take a cow or a goat, split it right down the middle, and lay the two halves out against each other. You would see two legs and half a brain on this side and two legs and half a brain on that side, and a big, bloody mess.

Then the candidates would stand back to back, in the middle of the laid out animal pieces, and they would walk a figure eight. One would walk around one side and then walk around the other side, signifying that, "All that I have is mixed with all that is yours." The other partner would do the same starting on the other side, and the two, having walked completely around the animal pieces on both sides, would come together face to face. That figure they walked is the current day numeral eight which, turned on its side, is also the symbol for infinity. That symbol has no beginning and no end.

Step number four is something we still do in our culture today, just without the cutting the part. The partners would cut the palms of their hands and mix their blood by shaking hands. Have you ever said, "Let's shake on it?" That action comes from the blood covenant ritual. Mixing their blood was the essence of step number four.

Step number five involved hot coals from a fire which was already blazing. The partners would take the hot ashes and rub them onto their palms to cauterize the wounds, creating a scar that would forever mark them as being in covenant. Similar to the wearing of wedding rings, whoever saw the scar would immediately recognize that the person in front of them was in covenant with somebody. So I knew that, if I was going to cheat you or fight you, I was going to have to deal with your covenant partner somewhere down the line.

Step number six was the exchange of names. Each party took on a covenant name. We still do this step when people get married; the wife takes a name that lets the world know that she is in covenant with a man.

Immediately following the name exchange, the seventh step would happen, which still takes place in the wedding ceremony. The covenant partners would recite the terms of the covenant, or the vows of the covenant. "All my enemies are all your enemies. All that you have is mine, and everything that I have is yours: all my assets, all my debts, all my friends, all my family, all my unborn children. It's all community property. Whether we're prosperous or not so much, whether with are healthy or not so much, in good times and in tough times, this covenant is binding." Marriage is the closest thing we have to the blood covenant of ancient times, and in fact, it's the last remaining blood covenant left in modern society.

The eighth step should sound a little familiar to church-going folks. Remember, the partners were pagans, pagan people that did not worship God. They worshipped the sun god, the moon god, the god of the sea, the god of war, and all kind of crazy, made-up nonsense. The partners brought out a meal, a memorial meal to settle the whole thing, a meal made up of bread and wine. The bread signified: "I am eating your flesh, and you're eating mine. I then drink your blood, the wine, and you drink mine. You are now on the inside of me, and I'm on the inside of you so that we are one flesh." The thinking sounds gross, but it was the pagan way of sealing the deal.

The ninth and final step was to go out and plant a tree and sprinkle the animal's blood on it. Remember the animals that were cut up, laid out, and walked between in step three? The partners gathered the blood they had spilled and sprinkled it on this freshly planted tree to mark the covenant they had made with each other. As the tree grew, it would serve as an everlasting sign of the covenant, and that the covenant would grow and get stronger with each passing year and generation.

God Finds a Guy

In Genesis 12, God met a guy that He believed could enter into a covenant with Him, and that guy was Abram. God waited a thousand years between Adam and Noah, and then another thousand years between Noah and Abram. Two thousand years had passed on the planet since God promised Adam that He would send a redeemer, someone to come save man and get the planet back out of Satan's hands. Finally, after two thousand years, God spotted someone He believed had the fortitude and character to be His covenant partner.

Now the LORD had said unto Abram, Get thee out of thy country, and from thy

kindred, and from thy father's house, unto a land that I will shew thee: and I will make of thee a great nation, and I will bless thee, and make thy name great; and thou shalt be a blessing: and I will bless them that bless thee, and curse him that curseth thee: and in thee shall all families of the earth be blessed.

Genesis 12:1-3

God introduced Himself to this guy, who was a worshipper of the moon god. He offered Abram a really great incentive package to leave his pagan worshipping ways and to start a relationship with Him, the one true God. People ask how Abram could be a worshipper of the moon god. The moon god was the patron god of Haran, the city where Abram and his family lived; that patronage was why God told him to leave his country, his kindred, and his father's entire house. If Abram had stayed, he would never have been able to make a clean break and worship only God. Further proof of this weakness is when Jacob's wife Rachel stole the gods from

her father when she left with Jacob. Rachel's father
Laban was from Abram's father's house.

**So Abram departed, as the LORD had
spoken unto him; and Lot went with him:
and Abram was seventy and five years
old when he departed out of Haran.**

Genesis 12:4

Abram was messing up already. God told him
to leave his entire father's house and all of his
relatives. Abram said all right to God, and then he
brought his nephew with him, who brought plenty
of trouble along. Let's not be too hard on Abram,
though, for half obeying God; we do it all the time.

**And Abram took Sarai his wife, and Lot
his brother's son, and all their substance
that they had gathered, and the souls
that they had gotten in Haran; and they
went forth to go into the land of Canaan;
and into the land of Canaan they came.
And Abram passed through the land unto**

the place of Sichem, unto the plain of Moreh. And the Canaanite was then in the land. And the LORD appeared unto Abram, and said, Unto thy seed will I give this land: and there builded he an altar unto the LORD, who appeared unto him.

Genesis 12:5-7

God and Abram started this relationship. Abram was not perfect or even close, but he was someone that God could work with in completing a covenant, the covenant. God began dating Abram, if you will; they were dating each other. Abram was seventy-five when he left for the new country of Canaan; however, a famine is in that land. Abram decided to go to Egypt, because they had food there.

Abram was married to a gal named Sarai, and she was a smoking hot chick. She was sixty-five years old and so smoking hot that Abram said, "Hey, Baby, let's lie. If the Egyptians find out that you're my wife, they'll kill me and take you for themselves; so let's say that you are my sister."

This lie is half true because Abram is Sarai's half-brother; they have the same daddy. Apparently Haran was like that movie *Deliverance* where your wife is your sister, but whatever. Back to the story at hand: Sarai was a total babe. They got to Egypt, and Abram said, "Hey, folks! This is my sister." Word spread about this new gorgeous girl in town, and Pharaoh got to Sarai, asked her to come home with him, and put her in the harem.

Pharaoh, being the gentleman that he was, commanded all of his subjects to do business with Abram and give him great deals on the trade. Pharaoh was wooing Abram for Sarai's hand in marriage, and Abram and Lot were getting filthy, nasty, Donald Trump rich out of the deal. Meanwhile, Sarai was not suffering; she was at the spa, getting facials, massages, manicures, pedicures, all in Pharaoh's harem, having a great time. Who wouldn't like spa days every day?

Pharaoh found out the real deal, that Sarai and Abram were married. How did he find out? God struck his entire house with a plague; some manuscripts say it was leprosy. Pharaoh got naturally and rightfully angry with Abram and kicked him out of the country. He commanded his army to escort them to the border and make sure they didn't come back. Abram, Sarai, and Lot left with all their possessions, and oh, by the way, they were very, very rich. *Were they just spiritually rich, Andrew?* Well, let's see what the Bible says.

And Abram went up out of Egypt, he, and his wife, and all that he had, and Lot with him, into the south. And Abram was very rich in cattle, in silver, and in gold.

Genesis 13:1-2

The whole crew went back to Bethel and Ai, and Lot and Abram were out in the countryside. They have servants and cattle and other livestock, but they have so much that they are butting heads. Lot's ranch hands are fighting with Abram's ranch hands. Abram tells Lot they shouldn't be fighting because they are family (side bar here: if Abram had fully obeyed God, Lot wouldn't be there, and there wouldn't be any fighting).

Abram offered Lot a pick of the choicest part of the land, and Abram would settle in the opposite direction. Lot looked around into the valley of the Jordan, and there off in the distance he spied San Francisco and Amsterdam, I mean Sodom and Gomorrah. That land looked really great; so he set up shop near those two seaside towns, and Abram went to the other side of the county.

Everyone was happy. Some time passed, and during this time period, nine kings were ruling the surrounding area. Four of the kings had been oppressing the other five for twelve years, and the five had finally had enough. The five kings got together in the thirteenth year and rebelled against the four, starting a war, which was not a good plan, because the four kings wiped out the five cities of the five kings. You guessed it: Sodom and Gomorrah were two of the five cities that got wiped out, and Lot and his family, along with all his possessions, were carried off. The four kings captured all of the provisions of each city, all the wealth of five cities, and they left.

One servant of Lot escaped, and he showed up to Abram's tent and told the story of Lot's capture. Abram gathered together all of his menservants, all of the ranch hands, the posse, the hired guns, and rallied up three hundred eighteen men. Those three hundred eighteen guys plus Abram, that's three hundred nineteen guys, made up the first commando team, because what they did was track down the armies of the four kings. Here were three hundred nineteen guys, which were equivalent to a reinforced company, against four armies, which were made up of between forty and a hundred thousand soldiers.

Three hundred nineteen ranch hands against a hundred thousand soldiers. Abram's unit arrived at night, and he split the group in two. Half went one way, and the other hundred and fifty went the other way. They made the first night raid recorded in all of history and routed the bad guys all the way back to Damascus. Abram's unit took everything back from the four kings (nine cities worth of wealth - not a bad day), and headed back home.

Surely you must realize that God's hand had to be in that victory, because three hundred nineteen country boys don't just beat a hundred thousand trained soldiers without help. Abram, feeling pretty good, was coming back with all that wealth and the freed prisoners taken as slaves and his boys whooping it up, when the catalyst to start the covenant ritual happened.

And Melchizedek king of Salem brought forth bread and wine: and he was the priest of the most high God.

Genesis 14:18

Salem was the ancient city of Jerusalem, and Melchizedek, the book of Hebrews tell us, was the preincarnate Jesus. He was a spirit being. God spent two thousand years looking for one man, a human, who could make a covenant with Him, and Abram, who is obviously not perfect, was who God chose. Here was Melchizedek, the priest of the most high God, already worshipping the true God, unlike Abram, who started out worshipping the moon god.

Why wouldn't God have picked Melchizedek instead of Abram? He couldn't, because Melchizedek was Jesus before He was Jesus the son of man. He was an eternal being, and God's covenant would not be legally binding for humans without a human to enter into the deal.

And he blessed him, and said, Blessed be Abram of the most high God, possessor of heaven and earth: and blessed be the most high God, which hath delivered thine enemies into thy hand. And he gave him tithes of all.

Genesis 14:19-20

Abram gave God ten percent of all the spoils. This gift is the first time anyone ever gave God a tithe, or ten percent. This giving on Abram's part was the flash point, the catalyst that allowed God to approach Abram and legally offer him a covenant. The very next thing recorded in Scripture was God showing up and beginning the covenant-cutting ritual with Abram. Ten years had gone by.

Abram finally gave to God, giving God the legal right to give to Abram, and God wastes no time in moving forward. Chapter 15 of Genesis records the beginning of the covenant ritual.

After these things the word of the LORD came unto Abram in a vision, saying, Fear not, Abram: I am thy shield, and thy exceeding great reward.

Genesis 15:1

Now that introduction sounds, on the surface, like a good deal. God's going to protect me ... blah, blah, blah ... reward. The truth is that God offers Abram here the first two steps of the blood covenant ritual. That word "shield" has the literal Hebrew meaning of the scaly hide of a crocodile. I have some crocodile skin boots; those things are tough and expensive. God must be doing all right for Himself if He has a full-length leather crocodile skin coat. He tells Abram, "I am that coat; I'm yours. The coat that I am is yours." God's giving Abram His coat; He's giving Abram His whole self.

God is saying, "I'm your shield. I'm your scaly hide of a crocodile."

The very next thing God says is, "I'm your exceeding great reward." That word "great" really means "an archer who shoots an arrow" in the Hebrew. The word "reward" is literally "victory". In the original language, the text reads like this: "I am your exceeding great archer that shoots an arrow to give you victory." So here is God saying to Abram, "I'll give you my coat, and I'll give you my weapons": steps one and two of the covenant ritual.

And Abram said, LORD God, what wilt thou give me, seeing I go childless, and the steward of my house is this Eliezer of Damascus? And Abram said, Behold, to me thou hast given no seed: and, lo, one born in my house is mine heir. And, behold, the word of the LORD came unto him, saying, This shall not be thine heir; but he that shall come forth out of thine own bowels shall be thine heir. And he brought him forth abroad, and said, Look

now toward heaven, and tell the stars, if thou be able to number them: and he said unto him, So shall thy seed be. And he believed in the LORD; and he counted it to him for righteousness.

Genesis 15:2-6

Abram believes God. "All right, God, You're going to give me a seed. You're going to give me a child; that is great." Abram is eighty-five years old at this time.

And he said unto him, I am the LORD that brought thee out of Ur of the Chaldees, to give thee this land to inherit it. And he said, LORD God, whereby shall I know that I shall inherit it?

Genesis 15:7-8

Abram is not out of faith. He doesn't disbelieve God, but he doesn't have the Bible. He's saying, "Great, You're giving me this land, but how is everybody else going to know it's mine?" God answers this very legitimate question from Abram.

And he said unto him, Take me an heifer of three years old, and a she goat of three years old, and a ram of three years old, and a turtledove, and a young pigeon. And he took unto him all these, and divided them in the midst, and laid each piece one against another: but the birds divided he not.

Genesis 15:9-10

Abram splits the animals right down the center, two legs on one side and two legs on the other. Abram knows what's going on. He was a pagan who worshipped the moon god, and this blood covenant was a pagan ritual. Abram recognizes step number three.

And when the fowls came down upon the carcasses, Abram drove them away. And when the sun was going down, a deep

sleep fell upon Abram; and, lo, an horror of great darkness fell upon him.

Genesis 15:11-12

We know from Galatians 3 that God was at the covenant cutting ritual, that Abraham was there, and that Christ was there, but now a fourth party shows up: a horror of great darkness. Horror and darkness have nothing to with God, but everything to do with Satan. Satan shows up, because he knows something is happening on planet earth, his planet, and he wants to find out what it is.

And it came to pass, that, when the sun went down, and it was dark, behold a smoking furnace, and a burning lamp that passed between those pieces.

Genesis 15:17

Abram sees what looks to him like a smoking furnace and a burning lamp, and he sees the furnace and the lamp walk the figure eight walk through the laid-out animal pieces. The smoking furnace is God the Father, because we know the burning lamp is Jesus Christ, the Son, the Light of the world, the Lamp unto my feet. The Father and the Son do the actual covenant walk. Jesus is Abraham's seed, and He stands in for Abraham to ensure that the covenant is confirmed. Jesus is in kind of a time warp. He shows up before His time as the physical seed of Abraham. People have a hard time wrapping their minds around that appearance, but remember that Jesus appears just prior to this passage as Melchizedek. Step number three of the blood covenant ritual is completed at this time. Abram wakes up and goes home. You would think he would run home all excited and tell Sarai about how he and God, the first Possessor of the heavens and the earth, cut a covenant, but things didn't go that way at home. (Have you ever been so excited when God revealed something to you that you wanted to share it with someone, and when you did, they just weren't that excited about it? Almost like it didn't even happen?) Welcome to Abram's world.

Now Sarai Abram's wife bare him no children: and she had an handmaid, an Egyptian, whose name was Hagar. And Sarai said unto Abram, Behold now, the LORD hath restrained me from bearing: I pray thee, go in unto my maid; it may be that I may obtain children by her. And Abram hearkened to the voice of Sarai.

Genesis 16:1-2

Apparently Hagar was a smoking hot chick, too, just a younger version, and she was Egyptian. Sarai told Abram to go sleep with Hagar so that they can get the promise of God of an heir. Sleeping with Hagar must have crossed Abram's mind before this suggestion, because he doesn't even ask Sarai, "Are you sure?" He says, "I think her light is still on," and he red rovers right on over to Hagar's tent and commences to "hearkening to Sarai's voice". Ishmael is born nine months later when Abram is eighty-six years old. Abram's name means "high father", or in modern English, "Mac Daddy". He's living the "Mac Daddy" life, too. When he walks into Egypt during the famine, he pimps out his wife to Pharaoh and gets filthy rich out of the deal. Now, he's got two smoking hot women and a son.

This guy for the next fourteen years doesn't think one thought about God or the covenant, because he has everything he wants. His biggest problem is keeping the two women from tearing each other's eyes out; other than that, he's good. He and Ishmael are going to Little League games together; they go bow hunting and do the monster truck rallies and the circus. He has his boy, his heir, and he's got two smoking hot chicks. He is living the Mac Daddy dream, and he doesn't give a rip about God or the covenant. Genesis doesn't record anything about Abram during this fourteen-year period. Abram's on auto pilot, and then...

And when Abram was ninety years old and nine, the LORD appeared to Abram, and said unto him, I am the Almighty God; walk before me, and be thou perfect.

Genesis 17:1

God has already completed three of the nine steps of the covenant ritual. Fourteen years go by, and God shows up and tells Abram, "Look, I'm God Almighty. I started this covenant with you, and I'm going to finish it. You better straighten up and fly right." Abram doesn't care about the promise; he thinks he already has the promise in Ishmael.

And I will make my covenant between me and thee, and will multiply thee exceedingly. And Abram fell on his face: and God talked with him, saying.

Genesis 17:2-3

Jinkies, Scoob, ruht-roh! If God showed up and told me to knock it off, I'd fall on my face, too. All of the sudden the reality hit Abram, "Whoops, the covenant God started with me fourteen years ago".

As for me, behold, my covenant is with thee, and thou shalt be a father of many nations. Neither shall thy name any more be called Abram, but thy name shall be

**Abraham; for a father of many nations
have I made thee.**

Genesis 17:4-5

Here God is picking up the covenant ritual
with step number six, the taking on of covenant
names. God tricks Abram into saying the promise
by changing his name to the promise, "I'll make
you the father of many nations." Abram's been
introducing himself as "Mac Daddy"; now every
time he introduces himself, he's saying, "I'm the
father of many nations", which is exactly what
the name Abraham means. God gives Abram a
new covenant name, Abraham, and God takes on
the name of Abraham. God is still known to this
day as the God of Abraham (as well as Isaac and
Jacob, which God added to His name as the covenant line progressed).

**And I will make thee exceeding fruitful,
and I will make nations of thee, and
kings shall come out of thee.**

Genesis 17:6

God launches into step number seven, the reciting of the terms of the covenant. God tells Abraham all the stuff that He going to do for him as part of the covenant. Let me add a sidebar really quickly here: "and kings shall come out of thee." Christ is Abraham's seed, who is obviously a King, the King of kings. We who are in Christ are also Abraham's seed, by faith, and Revelation says that we are all kings and priests. God is talking about us right here in the terms of the covenant. He is talking about us as the kings that come out of Abraham.

Abraham is trying to get his mind around all of the promises God is reciting as part of the covenant, and we'll see later on in Genesis 17 that Abraham is not really buying it. He's having a hard time with God's plan. Don't judge him too harshly; we have all been there, if we're honest about things.

And I will establish my covenant between me and thee and thy seed after thee in their generations for an everlasting

covenant, to be a God unto thee, and to thy seed after thee. And I will give unto thee, and to thy seed after thee, the land wherein thou art a stranger, all the land of Canaan, for an everlasting posses- sion; and I will be their God. And God said unto Abraham, Thou shalt keep my covenant therefore, thou, and thy seed after thee in their generations. This is my covenant, which ye shall keep, between me and you and thy seed after thee; every man child among you shall be circumcised.

Genesis 17:7-10

This circumcision is step number five, the sign of being in covenant, the scar. Remember, step six is taking on covenant names, and step seven is reciting the terms of the covenant. Now we see step five. Instead of cutting the palm of the hand and rubbing hot ashes into the wound to create a scar, which would've seemed like a better deal to me, God says to Abraham, circumcise yourself.

And ye shall circumcise the flesh of your foreskin; and it shall be a token of the covenant betwixt me and you. And he that is eight days old shall be circumcised among you, every man child in your generations, he that is born in the house, or bought with money of any stranger, which is not of thy seed. He that is born in thy house, and he that is bought with thy money, must needs be circumcised: and my covenant shall be in your flesh for an everlasting covenant. And the uncircumcised man child whose flesh of his foreskin is not circumcised, that soul shall be cut off from his people; he hath broken my covenant. And God said unto Abraham, As for Sarai thy wife, thou shalt not call her name Sarai, but Sarah shall her name be. And I will bless her, and give thee a son also of her: yea, I will bless her, and she shall be a mother of nations; kings of people shall be of her. Then Abraham fell upon his

**face, and laughed, and said in his heart,
Shall a child be born unto him that is an
hundred years old? and shall Sarah, that
is ninety years old, bear? And Abraham
said unto God, O that Ishmael might live
before thee!**

Genesis 17:11-18

Abraham is saying, "Hey God, that's some
crazy stuff you're talking there, but I already have
my boy." Is Abraham walking in faith here? Does
he believe God? He's laughing at God, for crying
out loud. Abraham is one hundred percent **NOT**
believing God! He has not bought into this thing
yet, although God has completed steps one, two,
three, six, seven and given the instructions for
number five, and Abraham is backing out.

For two thousand years, God has searched for
a man He can enter into covenant with to get the
Redeemer here. Then He finds a guy, invests ten
more years into getting to know him, and starts
the covenant ritual. Then the guy goes off and tries
to get the promise on his own (I know we've never

done that), which sidetracks the deal for fourteen more years. Finally, God has a sit down with His covenant guy, and the guy laughs in His face and says, "No thanks, I've already got the promise of an heir, Ishmael, and I'm already emotionally attached. I don't want a different heir, a supernatural heir. I'm too old and set in my ways, and my wife is too old to have kids. I'm good, thanks."

If God doesn't get this process back on track, He'll have to start all over, and the first guy took over two thousand years.

And God said, Sarah thy wife shall bear thee a son indeed; and thou shalt call his name Isaac: and I will establish my covenant with him for an everlasting covenant, and with his seed after him. And as for Ishmael, I have heard thee: behold, I have blessed him, and will make him fruitful, and will multiply him exceedingly; twelve princes shall he beget, and I will make him a great nation. But my covenant will I establish with Isaac, which Sarah shall

bear unto thee at this set time in the next year. And he left off talking with him, and God went up from Abraham.

Genesis 17:19-22

God says to Abraham, "I'll take care of Ishmael; don't worry about him. But the covenant line is coming through Isaac. The child that I give you through Sarah (God gave her a covenant name too) is the one that is going to be your only son. You will have to divorce yourself from Ishmael and make him a bastard, but I'll bless him and take care of him.

And Abraham took Ishmael his son, and all that were born in his house, and all that were bought with his money, every male among the men of Abraham's house; and circumcised the flesh of their foreskin in the selfsame day, as God had said unto him. And Abraham was ninety years old and nine, when he was circumcised in the flesh of his foreskin. And

Ishmael his son was thirteen years old, when he was circumcised in the flesh of his foreskin. In the selfsame day was Abraham circumcised, and Ishmael his son. And all the men of his house, born in the house, and bought with money of the stranger, were circumcised with him.

Genesis 17:23-27

I think Abraham probably didn't do himself first, because he would have been hurting pretty bad. I want you to think *Survivor,* here. This guy has a flint knife doing surgery on himself and Ishmael and the three hundred eighteen guys who helped bring back Lot. Remember the commandos? "Hey guys, meet me behind the woodshed at 1300 hours. Oh, and you won't need your weapons. Just put them in the armory, and report to me." There was no going down to St. Luke's and getting anesthesia or even ice packs.

Abraham wasn't walking in faith when he laughed at God, but I'm telling you, he was in faith here one hundred percent! If he didn't buy into this whole thing, if he didn't believe God, do you really think he would cut himself in the prescribed location? I wouldn't. And he had to talk all those other cats, the three hundred eighteen commandos, into getting cut. This guy was persuasive. He had to believe.

Abraham was eighty-five years old when steps one, two, and three of the covenant were completed. He was ninety-nine years old when steps five, six, and seven were completed. Let's fast forward to the birth of Isaac.

And the LORD visited Sarah as he had said, and the LORD did unto Sarah as he had spoken. For Sarah conceived, and bare Abraham a son in his old age, at the set time of which God had spoken to him. And Abraham called the name of his son that was born unto him, whom Sarah bare to him, Isaac. And Abraham circumcised his son Isaac being eight days old, as God had commanded him.

And Abraham was an hundred years old, when his son Isaac was born unto him.

Genesis 21:1-5

Here's the time line. Abraham was ninety-nine years old when he finally got into faith, really believed God, and circumcised himself and all the males in his household, and exactly one year later Isaac was born. All my life, I've heard preachers say, "Abraham had to wait twenty-five years for the promise; so hold on, and press on. You have to wait a long time for God to fulfill His promises." Well, Abraham didn't actually get into faith and start acting on the promise until he cut himself with that flint knife.

Abraham got the promise one year after circumcising himself, and Sarah was pregnant for nine months. Nine months subtracted from twelve months leaves three months, or roughly twelve weeks. After Abraham did surgery on himself, figure in about six weeks to recover before Abe and Sarah head off to the honeymoon tent. That leaves about a six-week window of time.

Every time that my wife was pregnant (we have three kids), we didn't find out for six weeks. I'm telling you, the first time Abraham and Sarah got together after he finally got into faith, she became pregnant with Isaac. He took six weeks to get the promise and six more weeks to realize he had it. Receiving the promise doesn't take long with God; it doesn't take twenty-five years. When you move, God will move right there with you. He was waiting on Abraham for twenty-five years, not the other way around. God waited and searched for two thousand years to find Abraham. He was not making Abraham wait; that idea is absurd.

Why Did God Ask Abraham to Sacrifice Isaac?

AFTER THESE events, God tested and proved Abraham and said to him, Abraham! And he said, Here I am. [God] said, Take now your son, your only son Isaac, whom you love, and go to the region of Moriah; and offer him there as

**a burnt offering upon one of the moun-
tains [which is Calvary] of which I will
tell you.**

Genesis 22:1-2 (AMP)

People say that this sacrifice was Abraham's
great test of faith. This was **NOT** a test of faith!
He already had the promise, an heir. He already
had it. Circumcising himself was the test of faith.
God was calling in a covenant marker. This sacrifice was not about faith but about reciprocity. The
blood covenant was reciprocal. When I gave to you,
my covenant partner, you could legally give back
to me. God couldn't give to you unless you gave
to Him first, because Satan legally was the god of
the world. Gad had no legal right to be involved in
anything on planet earth unless a human invited
Him to intervene in his life.

Isaac was not a child. He was between thirty
and thirty-seven years old when this event took
place. I believe he was around thirty-three,
because who else was sacrificed at about thirty-
three years of age? Jesus. Isaac was between

thirty and thirty-seven; we know this much from Scripture. He wasn't some ten-year-old kid, like we saw in Sunday school lesson books. He was a man. *(For more in depth study on Abraham and Isaac go to www.thecloc.com "Audio Archives" page and download the MP3 files on the "El Shaddai" from The Character of God series.)*

Abraham was in faith. He was already experiencing the full benefits of the covenant, riches, honor and life, because he was about one hundred thirty-three years old at the time. He had the heir he was promised; so this sacrifice was definitely not a faith test. God was calling in a covenant marker. God was saying here, "I've given you everything that I have. So you have to give me everything that you have, and now it's time to pony up." Why did God ask for Isaac? Was He nuts? Human sacrifice? Everywhere else, the Bible clearly stated, NO HUMAN SACRIFICE! What was going on here?

God needed to a have a covenant partner, a man, a human who had a legal right to be on the earth, to give Him his only son so that God could give that covenant partner, that man, that human who had legal right to be on the earth, His only Son, Jesus. This point is so technical, but God could **NOT** give Jesus to Abraham until Abraham gave Isaac to God.

Let me say again that God had to find somebody on the planet who would give Him his only son so that God could give that man His only Son. Now, Jesus came for the whole of mankind, but God legally gave Jesus to Abraham and to the seed of Abraham after him. God gave Christ to Abraham. He couldn't give Jesus to Abraham until Abraham gave Him Isaac. That exchange was the entire reason for cutting the blood covenant. It was man's covenant. It was a pagan ritual. Remember, the partners say to one another, "If you give me everything that you have, I can give you everything that I have. Not only can I give you everything, but legally I have to give to you in reciprocity." This legal arrangement is the only way God could get the Redeemer onto the planet legally and break Satan's hold over the earth and mankind. It's all very technically legal, but God

went to great lengths in order to give us everything that now belongs to us, which is riches,
honor, and life.

**So Abraham rose early in the morning,
saddled his donkey, and took two of his
young men with him and his son Isaac;
and he split the wood for the burnt
offering, and then began the trip to the
place of which God had told him. On the
third day Abraham looked up and saw
the place in the distance. And Abraham
said to his servants, Settle down and
stay here with the donkey, and I and the
young man will go yonder and worship
and come again to you.**

Genesis 22:3-5 (AMP)

People say to me, "See, Andrew, it says 'young
man' right there in the Bible." Well, if you were a
hundred and thirty three years old and you were
hiking up a mountain with a thirty-three-year-old
man, you'd call that guy a young man, too.

Then Abraham took the wood for the burnt offering and laid it on [the shoulders of] Isaac his son, and he took the fire (the firepot) in his own hand, and a knife; and the two of them went on together. And Isaac said to Abraham, My father! And he said, Here I am, my son. [Isaac] said, See, here are the fire and the wood, but where is the lamb for the burnt sacrifice? Abraham said, My son, God Himself will provide a Lamb for the burnt offering. So the two went on together. When they came to the place of which God had told him, Abraham built an altar there; then he laid the wood in order and bound Isaac his son and laid him on the altar on the wood. And Abraham stretched forth his hand and took hold of the knife to slay his son. But the Angel of the Lord called to him from heaven and said, Abraham, Abraham! He answered, Here I am.

Genesis 22:6-11 (AMP)

If Abraham wasn't listening, boy-howdy, Isaac was smoked. The knife was coming down, and the Angel of the Lord called his name twice. Abraham stopped in mid-stab, heard, and obeyed.

And He said, Do not lay your hand on the lad or do anything to him; for now I know that you fear and revere God, since you have not held back from Me or begrudged giving Me your son, your only son.

Genesis 22:12 (AMP)

Notice the language that God uses here in describing Isaac. It's very similar to the language in John 3:16; Abraham gave God his only son.

Then Abraham looked up and glanced around, and behold, behind him was a ram caught in a thicket by his horns. And Abraham went and took the ram and offered it up for a burnt offering and an ascending sacrifice instead of his son! So Abraham called the name of that place

The Lord Will Provide. And it is said to this day, On the mount of the Lord it will be provided. The Angel of the Lord called to Abraham from heaven a second time And said, I have sworn by Myself, says the Lord, that since you have done this and have not withheld [from Me] or begrudged [giving Me] your son, your only son.

Genesis 22:13-16 (AMP)

Abraham stuck with the covenant. God called in the covenant marker, and Abraham willingly, without hesitation, anted up and gave God his only begotten son.

In blessing I will bless you and in multiplying I will multiply your descendants like the stars of the heavens and like the sand on the seashore. And your Seed (Heir) will possess the gate of His enemies, and in your Seed [Christ] shall all the nations of the earth be blessed and

[by Him] bless themselves, because you have heard and obeyed My voice.

Genesis 22:17-18 (AMP)

We have the advantage of looking back at this scene. Paul gives us a snapshot of it, looking back at this very incident with the benefit of a couple thousand years of hindsight.

By faith Abraham, when he was tried, offered up Isaac: and he that had received the promises offered up his only begotten son, of whom it was said, That in Isaac shall thy seed be called: accounting that God was able to raise him up, even from the dead; from whence also he received him in a figure.

Hebrews 11:17-19

The final word in verse 19, "figure", literally means in the Greek, similitude or image. Paul tells us exactly what happened that day on Calvary. They didn't have DVDs or VCRs, but they knew a figure or image. They didn't have cameras, but they had paintings and portraits. Don't you know that heaven has some really advanced technology? We haven't even started to scratch the surface with our advancements.

Back to Paul's analysis: HNN, Heavenly News Network, came down and had the camera crew set up over Mount Calvary that day four thousand years ago, when Abraham and Isaac hiked up there. They were filming the scene, with Isaac on the altar and Abraham bringing the knife down, when suddenly the angel said, "Stop! It's good Abraham, we got it." The sacrifice scene was a wrap, and the angels took that DVD of all that happened that day and put it in the vault in heaven. That DVD was safely stored in the vault until the end of the age, when there will be a trial.

Satan is going to say, "No, no, no! All these people have to go to hell with me because Jesus had no right to be here. He was here illegally. His sacrifice doesn't count." God will say, "Nope, here's the covenant." The angels will pull out that DVD, and they will play back all of those nine steps of the covenant ritual. God will show Abraham giving his only begotten son to God, not withholding anything, so that God could give Jesus to Abraham. What happened was all legal and a done deal. What happened that day, the reason why God asked Abraham to put Isaac on that altar and to sacrifice him, was to fulfill the covenant.

That DVD in the vault in heaven will come out at the end of the ages as evidence as to why you and I can have eternal life! Glory! I love this stuff!

What About the Missing Steps of the Covenant Ritual?

If you think back, you'll remember that God only completed six of the nine covenant ritual steps. God only completed six steps with Abraham. So I began to pray about the final and missing three steps. I've never heard taught before what I'm about to lay out, but I asked, "Father, this covenant thing, you know I've heard the experts on this subject teach that you didn't have to complete all nine steps. Why would you go to all the lengths to make everything completely airtight and legally binding but not complete all nine steps? Why would you just do some of them?"

The answer came quickly, as it always does when I ask the right questions. Most of us are so focused on the wrong things that we get bogged down with what Jesus called "the cares of this life". What comes next is the answer through which the Holy Spirit led me, and once you see it, you'll think it's so simple that a five year old could get it.

Remember, God put the law, the old covenant, into effect as a band-aid, a stopgap measure. What He was doing was giving Himself enough time to complete the last three steps of the covenant ritual. The first three steps were done when Abraham was eighty-five years old. Fourteen years went by, and Abraham was ninety-nine years old when the next steps occurred. So the steps don't have to be done at the same time. God put the old covenant, the law, in place until He could buy Himself enough time to get Jesus here as a man, a human, to complete the last three steps.

The three steps that Abraham did not complete were steps number four, eight, and nine. Step four was the mixing of the covenant partners' blood. God's blood had to be mixed with man's blood. Step number eight was the meal of bread and wine. Finally, step nine was to plant a tree and sprinkle blood on it.

The book of the generation of Jesus Christ, the son of David, the son of Abraham.

Matthew 1:1

Matthew goes through a bunch of verses which show the covenant lineage, "So and so begat so and so, and so and so begat so and so." Those verses document legally how God mixed His blood with Abraham's to produce the Seed, Christ, all the way to a virgin teenage girl named Mary.

Now the birth of Jesus Christ was on this wise: When as his mother Mary was espoused to Joseph, before they came

together, she was found with child of the Holy Ghost. Then Joseph her husband, being a just man, and not willing to make her a public example, was minded to put her away privily. But while he thought on these things, behold, the angel of the LORD appeared unto him in a dream, saying, Joseph, thou son of David, fear not to take unto thee Mary thy wife: for that which is conceived in her is of the Holy Ghost.

Matthew 1:18-20

I don't really mean to have a sex education class here, but when a female gets pregnant, a sperm and an egg have to come together before conception occurs. Verse 20 states in no uncertain terms that Jesus was conceived of the Holy Spirit. God's sperm fertilizes Mary's egg. God mixes His blood that day with man's blood. He doesn't cut His palm and shake hands; because God is a spirit, to do the handshake and mix blood would be pretty hard. God's a creative guy, and He comes up with a way to mix His blood with Abraham's by the Immaculate Conception. For that reason, the Virgin Birth is pivotal to being a Christian; without it; there is no legally binding covenant. Without mixing blood, the whole thing is null and void. Jesus is the firstborn of us all who have eternal (perpetual) life; Jesus has both God's DNA and man's DNA on the inside of Him. So He called Himself both the Son of God and the Son of Man.

The Holy Spirit is Jesus' physical father, and God is His spiritual father. The same happens for us when we are born of the spirit or born again. God becomes our spiritual father, and the Holy Spirit adopts us as His physical children. That process is the "Spirit of Adoption". We have human fathers, but the Holy Spirit adopts us as His children. And that reason is why Jesus said to "call no human your father". We become new creatures, or that new species of being as the Greek says, and what ties into the covenant is that God mixed His blood with man so that by faith we become a part of Him supernaturally. Step number four is complete.

Step number eight is the pagan meal of bread and wine, which is going to signify cannibalism. "I'm eating your flesh, and you are eating my flesh. I'm drinking your blood, and you are drinking my blood." Saying so sounds creepy. It is creepy, but it's man's covenant, invented by pagans. God always meets us on whatever level we are on, and that pagan ritual is the playing field where He had to meet Abraham. You all know where this one is going, right?

And as they were eating, Jesus took bread, and blessed it, and brake it, and gave it to the disciples, and said, Take, eat; this is my body. And he took the cup, and gave thanks, and gave it to them, saying, Drink ye all of it; for this is my blood of the new testament, which is shed for many for the remission of sins.

Matthew 26:26-28

The memorial meal of bread and wine, step number eight, communion, the Lord's Supper, or the Eucharist, does not symbolize Jesus' death. It is the one step of the covenant ritual that we get to do. Jesus instituted communion in order to give us an equal part in the covenant ritual with the Father, Abraham, and Himself. When you take communion, you are taking your place at the table as an equal partner in the blood covenant ritual. If you'll look back to Genesis 14, you'll notice that Melchizedek, preincarnate Jesus, brought out to Abraham a meal of bread and wine and that they enjoyed communion before God started the covenant ritual.

The final step, number nine, was to plant a tree and sprinkle blood on it as a permanent symbol of the freshly completed covenant.

Christ hath redeemed us from the curse of the law, being made a curse for us: for it is written, Cursed is every one that hangeth on a tree.

Galatians 3:13

The cross to which Jesus was nailed is that covenant tree, planted in the same exact spot where Abraham gave Isaac to God two thousand years prior. In Jesus, God gives back to Abraham His only Son, and He sprinkles His only Son's blood on that covenant tree, the cross of Calvary.

After this, Jesus knowing that all things were now accomplished, that the scripture might be fulfilled, saith, I thirst. Now there was set a vessel full of vinegar: and they filled a sponge with vinegar, and put it upon hyssop, and put it to his mouth. When Jesus therefore had received the vinegar, he said, It is finished: and he bowed his head, and gave up the ghost.

John 19:28-30

What is finished? What are the "all things" that were now accomplished? I've heard preachers say, "Oh, the old covenant is finished," or "The payment of sin was finished." No. No. NO! With step number nine, God planted the tree and sprinkled the blood of the Lamb on it, and the blood covenant ritual is finished. All the things accomplished are all nine steps. The covenant that God had set out to make with Abraham is finally finished. The new covenant Jesus discussed means, "freshly completed covenant", not new as opposed to old, but new as in freshly completed. The covenant partners Abraham, God, and Christ, who did the covenant figure-eight walk two thousand years prior, finished it. So Jesus can truly say that it is finished.

What we in Christianity today call the "new covenant" is really the covenant. The over-arching covenant that was started in the Garden of Eden with the promise of the Seed, before the law ever was given, before the old covenant, before the band-aid, is finally finished. And it is sealed forever with the blood of Jesus, and that ritual is legally why we can have riches, honor, and life. All of this treasure comes to us because Abraham was (oh, man, thank God for that guy) willing and obedient. I have three kids. I can't give any of them up. Could you imagine giving up yours? How much does God love us to go through with this ritual? How great was Abraham's faith and character? My God is so good! That sacrifice shows how much He loves us. That gift is why the covenant is unbreakable. If you are going through sickness or troubled relationships or you can't pay your bills, that AIN'T the covenant. God is not withholding any good thing from you, not any good thing. Those fifteen components of evil (adversity, affliction, calamity, displeasure, distress [WORRY], exceeding great grief, harm, heaviness, hurt, ill favor [when somebody doesn't like you], misery, sadness, sorrow, trouble, and wrong) come straight out of hell. Satan tried to throw them on Abraham when a darkness of horror came upon him, but thank God, he broke through them. Abraham pushed through the darkness.

For a long time, he was oppressed, depressed, and alone in the darkness. It was a great horror. And then, when Abraham looked up, he saw the Father and Son come and walk the covenant walk through those animal pieces. No, God is not with-holding one good thing from us. He went to way too much trouble to make sure that He could get riches, honor, and life into our hands.

He that spared not his own Son, but deliv-ered him up for us all, how shall he not with him also freely give us all things?
Romans 8:32

Please don't blame God for any bad thing going on in your life. He's not trying to teach you some-thing. Your misfortune is not His will for you, and it's not your lot in life. Riches, and honor, and life are the covenant, and if anything in your life comes along that is outside of those three cate-gories (riches, honor, and life), it's NOT your cov-enant. It's NOT from God, and it's straight out of the pits of hell.

CHAPTER 3

Back From the Dark Side

In the first chapter, we talked about *Covenant for Rookies*, the covenant summed up in three words; riches, honor and life. In the second chapter, we learned about the ancient covenant ritual, and why and how God ensured we could legally have riches, honor, and life. I'm sure you've noticed that riches, honor, and life don't just fall on you like gold falls on Scrooge McDuck. Have you ever wondered why bad things happen to good Christian people? Maybe you've even wondered why bad things have happened in your life. But then you figured God must be trying to build your character or try you by fire, or maybe you think you don't measure up. You then replay all the mistakes and on-purpose-bad-decisions you've made in your life, and those foul ups explain why bad stuff has happened to you.

The guilt comes, and then you try to make up for it by doing the good checklist: go to church, pray every day and have your quiet time, feed the homeless, work in the nursery or usher, pay your tithes, and maybe even give some extra. You do all this work in an effort to assuage your guilt, get God off your back, and hopefully get good things to begin to happen to you. Well, at least some of the bad stuff might let up and give you a breather. But all your effort doesn't seem to work; so you ditch the bad checklist, "don't cuss, drink, smoke, or chew, or run around with those that do". The harder you try to keep both checklists, the worse things seem to get. Finally, you throw in the towel; you stop trying to keep the commandments, because you are exhausted. That method doesn't work very well, either. You are suddenly cognizant of all your new mistakes and "on purposes", and the cycle begins again as you climb back on the wagon of checklist keeping. Why is this cycle happening? Surely there's more to being a Christian than this fruitless struggle?

There is! Remember, you are in covenant. The Father gave Jesus, and Jesus gave Himself, so that we could have riches, honor, and life. *But how do I experience those things, Andrew?* I'm glad you asked.

And this I say, that the covenant, that was confirmed before of God in Christ, the law, which was four hundred and thirty years after, cannot disannul, that it should make the promise of none effect.

Galatians 3:17

The law, which we consider the old covenant, didn't show up until four hundred thirty years after God already cut covenant with Abraham. It came as an afterthought. It was not the original plan, but a band-aid, a stopgap measure. The law was not God's best plan for us. People have a hard time with the idea of God having to use a second option or backup plan. To clarify, let me ask: Was David God's first or second option? Was King David God's original plan?

David was God's third choice, third option, and plan number three. The original plan was for Israel to be a nation of priests with God as their King. The people rejected that idea; so God implemented plan number two. Saul was anointed king of Israel. He made a mess of the job, being disobedient and disloyal to God. Enter plan number three: David. God has to deal with people, which is why He took two thousand years to find Abraham to cut covenant. So let's not have a religious/traditional mindset when thinking about God, His character, and how He does things.

For if the inheritance be of the law, it is no more of promise: but God gave it to Abraham by promise.

Galatians 3:18

The law, the band-aid, started in Exodus 20, which is when God first gave the Ten

Commandments, and it extended all the way to the point in time when Jesus, the Seed, showed up, died on the cross, and said, "It is finished". At that point, we entered into what we call the new covenant. The total time the law was in effect was about fifteen hundred seventy years. That period of time is not a whole lot when you look at the entire six-thousand-year timeline of mankind on the planet. The law was in effect less than twenty percent of man's history with God, starting with Adam in the Garden, yet most of Christianity builds and bases itself on the law, the Ten Commandments. We are hanging onto the band-aid and forgetting the covenant, God's overall and original plan.

Wherefore then serveth the law? It was added because of transgressions, till the seed should come to whom the promise was made; and it was ordained by angels in the hand of a mediator.

Galatians 3:19

The apostle Paul clearly stated the purpose and duration of the law in this verse. It was to last in duration only until the Seed should come. Has the Seed, which is Christ, come? Of course He has. So why do we as Christians continue to cling to the law?

Further, Paul reveals why God gave us the law at all. He added it because of "transgressions", a word which literally means in the Greek, violations or the crossing of a boundary from one kingdom into another.

When I was in the Marine Corps and serving as a forward observer, I would use the following terms when talking to a pilot while calling in an airstrike: "Ingress", "Egress", and "Transgress". Ingress was the direction to the target. Egress was the direction away from the target. And transgress was when the plane crossed the target.

God gave the law because the children of Israel had transgressed or crossed the boundary from living inside the covenant (God's Ponderosa, remember?) to outside the covenant, into the kingdom of darkness or the devil's backyard. They crossed over into slavery for four hundred years in Egypt. Once God got them out, He gave Moses the law to lay out clear-cut boundary markers to keep them inside the covenant (on the Ponderosa) until Jesus was born.

This verse also speaks of the origin of the law. The King James says that it was ordained by the angels. We know that God gave the law to Moses face to face on Mount Sinai. So what does this phrase mean? If we search out the Greek, the word "ordained" means "by means of or mechanisms of" or "modeled".

What God did was to model the law after what the angels in heaven do. You know about the ark of the covenant and the mercy seat and all that Indiana Jones stuff. Well, they are models of the real ark and mercy seat in heaven. All the stuff the angels do in ministering to God in heaven serves as a model for what Moses passed down to the priests and the Levites. God ordained or modeled the law after the angel's duties, and verse 19 says that it was in the hands of a mediator.

The mediator was Moses. God gave the law to Moses, and Moses gave it to the people. This mediation was also not God's original plan. Read Exodus 18 and 19, and you'll see that God's original plan was to have no mediator, but a direct relationship with people. They were scared and set Moses up as the mediator. The funny thing is that a lot of Christians act the same way today with their ministers. They want a minister to be the mediator between themselves and God.

Now a mediator is not a mediator of one, but God is one.

Galatians 3:20

When we are born of the Spirit or born again, believing that what Jesus did was enough, we become part of the body of Christ. When God looks at us, He sees the person, Head and body, of Christ. As I said in the last chapter, when my friend Sam comes walking up to me, I say, "There's Sam." I don't say, "There's Sam's head on Julia's body." The body and the head are one person, are they not? Jesus is the Head, and we are the body. We are one with Christ; we are part of the person of Christ.

A mediator is a middleman between two or more parties. When the law was given, the parties consisted of God and the children of Israel, with Moses as the middleman. Since the finished work of Jesus, we are one with Him, one with God. We have no need for a mediator, no need for a middleman, any longer. You can go straight to God. You don't need a preacher or a pastor. You don't need a prophet or an apostle. You don't need to go through a ministry gift. You are one in Christ; so you don't need a mediator.

You have access to the throne of the Creator of the universe. You have the same power, authority or "juice" with God as any minister. You have the same rights and privileges as any pastor, prophet, apostle, teacher, evangelist, deacon, or elder. We are all kings and priests, not some kings and some priests. We are kings **and** priests, NOT kings **or** priests (see Revelation 1:6 and Revelation 5:10).

Is the law then against the promises of God? God forbid: for if there had been a law given which could have given life, verily righteousness should have been by the law. But the scripture hath concluded all under sin, that the promise by faith of Jesus Christ might be given to them that believe. But before faith came, we were kept under the law, shut up unto the faith which should afterwards be revealed. Wherefore the law was our schoolmaster to bring us unto Christ, that we might be justified by faith. But after that faith is come, we are no longer under a schoolmaster.

Galatians 3:21-25

We are no longer under the schoolmaster or the law. Paul again states, in more detail, that the law was a set of boundaries to mark the path to Christ. The band-aid existed to show people the way to the entrance of the covenant. By realizing we could never measure up, but by believing that

Jesus paid the bill in full, we enter into the covenant and become a part of the body of Christ.

The DARK Side of the Law

There is a dark side to the law. Remember that step number seven was to recite the terms of the covenant. In Genesis 17, when God recited the terms of the covenant to Abraham, He recited all good things. "All that I have is yours. You give me everything that you have, and life will be wonderful." Then violations started to come, transgressions, the crossing of the borders outside of the covenant. During the giving of the law, God spells out what happens when transgressions occur, because we as humans are kind of brainless. My kids say all the time after a transgression, "I didn't know". So God spells out all of the consequences, the dark side of the law, which is called the curse of the law in the Bible. Galatians 3:13 says, "Christ has redeemed us from the curse of the law." The dark side is called the curse of the law.

Most people in the body of Christ have never heard of the curse of the law, and the few that have often confuse the curse of the law with the curse of the fall. The two curses are completely different things. People are constantly asking me, as a pastor, "Why do bad things happen to good Christian people?" The reason is that we live under the curse of the fall. Christ hasn't yet redeemed us from the curse of the fall; He redeemed us from the curse of the law. So much misunderstanding and wrong thinking when bad things happen to good people depends on this error. The Word of God can shed light on these questions and provide clear-cut answers. To understand what's going on, we must understand both the curse of the fall and the curse of the law, the difference between them, and the covenant solution to overcoming bad stuff.

The Curse of the Fall

Now the serpent was more subtil than any beast of the field which the LORD

God had made. And he said unto the woman, Yea, hath God said, Ye shall not eat of every tree of the garden? And the woman said unto the serpent, We may eat of the fruit of the trees of the garden: but of the fruit of the tree which is in the midst of the garden, God hath said, Ye shall not eat of it, neither shall ye touch it, lest ye die. And the serpent said unto the woman, Ye shall not surely die: for God doth know that in the day ye eat thereof, then your eyes shall be opened, and ye shall be as gods, knowing good and evil. And when the woman saw that the tree was good for food, and that it was pleasant to the eyes, and a tree to be desired to make one wise, she took of the fruit thereof, and did eat, and gave also unto her husband <u>with her</u>; and he did eat. And the eyes of them both were opened, and they knew that they

were naked; and they sewed fig leaves together, and made themselves aprons.

Genesis 3:1-7

(emphasis mine)

Eve was deceived, but Adam willingly disobeyed God. Disobedience was his choice. Scripture says that he was right there with his wife and did nothing to stop her from being tricked. He made a freewill choice to disobey God. He sinned, not Eve, and then the curse of the fall happened.

I've heard preachers say, "Now God pronounced the curse." If you pronounce my name, "Andrew", you don't make me or bring me into existence. You are simply calling me by name. God in His mercy lets Adam and Eve know what just happened to them so that Adam won't be totally in the dark as to why everything is going wrong all of the sudden: e.g., realizing you are naked. God lets all three players in this drama know the results or consequences of their actions.

And they heard the voice of the LORD God walking in the garden in the cool of the day: and Adam and his wife hid themselves from the presence of the LORD God amongst the trees of the garden. And the LORD God called unto Adam, and said unto him, Where art thou? And he said, I heard thy voice in the garden, and I was afraid, because I was naked; and I hid myself. And he said, Who told thee that thou wast naked? Hast thou eaten of the tree, whereof I commanded thee that thou shouldest not eat? And the man said, The woman whom thou gavest to be with me, she gave me of the tree, and I did eat. And the LORD God said unto the woman, What is this that thou hast done? And the woman said, The serpent beguiled me, and I did eat. And the LORD God said unto the serpent, Because thou hast done this, thou art cursed above all cattle, and above every beast of the field; upon thy belly shalt thou go, and

dust shalt thou eat all the days of thy life: and I will put enmity between thee and the woman, and between thy seed and her seed; it shall bruise thy head, and thou shalt bruise his heel.

Genesis 3:8-15

(emphasis mine)

The first part of verse 15 is physically speaking. This first phase is in the natural realm, and we still "enjoy" this part today. I hate snakes. Snakes will bite me, they will bite my kids. Why? They behave that way because God put enmity between us and them.

The second half of verse 15 is supernatural; it switches over to that realm when God promises a Redeemer. Jesus is coming. God says, "It": it, it, it, the seed, singular. God used the same language with Abraham when speaking of Jesus; Christ was Abraham's seed, singular. "It shall bruise thy head, and thou shalt bruise his heel."

God is speaking directly to Lucifer. Do you think that very snake that was in the Garden that day was still around for another four thousand years until Jesus was crucified? Of course not: God is speaking to Lucifer and at the same time promising that a Redeemer is coming, someone to buy back the planet and restore nature to its original state, minus the curse.

Unto the woman he said, I will greatly multiply thy sorrow and thy conception; in sorrow thou shalt bring forth children; and thy desire shall be to thy husband, and he shall rule over thee. And unto Adam he said, Because thou hast hearkened unto the voice of thy wife, and hast eaten of the tree, of which I commanded thee, saying, Thou shalt not eat of it: cursed is the ground for thy sake; in sorrow shalt thou eat of it all the days of thy life; thorns also and thistles shall it bring forth to thee; and thou shalt eat the herb of the field.

Genesis 3:16-18

All the bad stuff that happens on planet earth happens because Adam willingly disobeyed God and turned all of the earth over to Satan. Did you notice where the curse went? It went into the ground. The curse went into the ground. Where do our bodies come from? Our bodies are made from the ground.

In the sweat of thy face shalt thou eat bread, till thou return unto <u>the ground;</u> <u>for out of it wast thou taken</u>: for dust thou art, and unto dust shalt thou return.

Genesis 3:19

(emphasis mine)

Why do our bodies age and decay? Why do we have to deal with sickness and degenerative diseases? Why does everything on this planet decay? Everything started eroding immediately after Adam delivered the earth to Satan.

The minute something is manufactured, it begins to decay, and anything manufactured comes out of the ground. Cars are made of materials that come out of the ground. Electronics are made of materials that come out of the ground. Furniture, clothes, housing, food, etc., all come out of the ground in some way, and manufacturers and sellers are always looking for ways to increase the time before decay takes over a product. Some products, like food, decay faster than others, like cars, but everything, including our bodies, decays (enter Botox).

The curse of the fall is why cars rust, why the plumbing gets stopped up, why the house needs repairs, and why we have to use Weed-B-Gone and Bug-Killer. Nature is out of kilter, not because God punished Adam, but because that was what happened when legal authority over nature went to Satan. This point is a no-brainer. When an evil guy like Hitler took over Germany, that country went downhill pretty fast. We can see in the natural realm that, when bad leaders are in charge, things go bad pretty quickly. For some reason, we check our brains at the door when dealing with spiritual things and blame God for bad stuff. That thinking is crazy.

The ground is cursed. All of nature is cursed. We have to deal with that reality every single day. Jesus said that the rain falls on the just and the unjust alike. Prior to the curse of the fall, there was no rain. There was no rain until Noah's flood. Christ did not redeem us from the curse of the fall; He redeemed us from the curse of the law. Don't get the two curses mixed up. Prior to the curse of the fall, nature and the earth all cooperated with man. What nature and earth did was to help mankind to produce wealth, food, provision, shelter, and everything he wanted or needed.

Remember that saying, "Money doesn't grow on trees"? Prior to the curse of the fall, it did. If you read Genesis, it says that gold was lying on the ground. You just reached down and picked it up. The planet was spitting this stuff out to man because it was in perfect harmony with him. There was not one thing that couldn't be accomplished between man and nature working together.

After the fall, man and nature began to compete with each other. Man had to work before, but no resistance hindered his work. God told Adam to tend the Garden and keep it. So man had to work in paradise; he wasn't just sitting on the beach sipping an umbrella drink. After Satan became the god of this world, man got the resistance, thorns and thistles, that produces the sweat of his brow. Man has to fight with nature to accomplish anything. Now we have strip mining and have to literally fight and wrestle the earth to get anything out of it. Drilling for oil is a major undertaking. Huge investments are involved in getting anything out of the earth. Producing anything takes blood, sweat and tears, all because of the curse of the fall.

Christ finally redeems us from the curse of the fall the second time He comes back. During His thousand-year reign, the curse of the fall greatly diminishes, and when God moves New Jerusalem to the earth afterwards, He completely eradicates the curse forever. I want to take you through some Scriptures that give us a snapshot of what our lives will look like sans the curse.

And there shall come forth a rod out of the stem of Jesse, and a Branch shall

grow out of his roots: and the spirit of the LORD shall rest upon him, the spirit of wisdom and understanding, the spirit of counsel and might, the spirit of knowledge and of the fear of the LORD; and shall make him of quick understanding in the fear of the LORD: and he shall not judge after the sight of his eyes, neither reprove after the hearing of his ears: but with righteousness shall he judge the poor, and reprove with equity for the meek of the earth: and he shall smite the earth: with the rod of his mouth, and with the breath of his lips shall he slay the wicked. And righteousness shall be the girdle of his loins, and faithfulness the girdle of his reins. The <u>wolf also shall dwell with the lamb,</u> and the leopard shall lie down with the kid; and the calf and the young lion and the fatling together; and a little child shall lead them. And the cow and the bear shall feed; their young ones shall lie down together: and the lion shall eat straw like the ox. And the sucking child shall play on the hole of the asp, and the weaned child shall put his hand on the cockatrice' den. They shall not hurt nor destroy in all my holy mountain: for the earth shall be full of the knowledge of the LORD, as the waters cover the sea. And in that day there shall be a root of Jesse, which shall stand for an ensign of the people; to it shall the Gentiles seek: and his rest shall be glorious.

Isaiah 11:1-10

(emphasis mine)

The wolf and lamb will be hanging out together, and the lion will eat grass, while the cow and bear play together. and a child will lead the pack. This picture describes when Jesus redeems us from the curse of the fall, when nature and mankind are back in harmony and working together, not competing.

For, behold, I create new heavens and a new earth: and the former shall not be remembered, nor come into mind.

Isaiah 65:17

I want to put this statement into the timeline for you to avoid confusion. The new heavens and a new earth spoken of here are translated into English incorrectly in light of the timeline that the Bible lays out for our future. We know that this promise is incorrectly translated, because the new heavens and new earth won't come until after the millennial reign of Jesus, immediately following the great tribulation period. The next thing that is going to happen on the prophetic timeline is the rapture or catching away of the church. All those who are born again will taken off the planet prior to the rise and reign of the "little horn", known in our culture today as the Antichrist, when all hell literally breaks loose on the planet for seven years.

Jesus comes back, bringing the saints (us) with Him and does the whole battle of Armageddon thing. He wipes out all the folks that picked Satan.

Those who live through the tribulation period and pick Jesus will continue to live physically in their natural bodies during the thousand year reign of Christ. They get to experience natural life on earth the way it was created and meant to be under the reversal of the curse of the fall. They get to live like Adam did before he sinned. The way I know this passage is speaking of the thousand year reign is that you will see that folks still died during this time.

The curse of the fall is still not completely eradicated until the very end of the age when Satan, who has been bound up during the thousand year reign, will be set free for one last season of time. He will actually convince some people to rebel and try one last time to overtake the throne. But alas, no dice, and God wins again.

At any rate, the Hebrew meaning of the phrase "the new heavens and a new earth" is "a new atmosphere and a new way". God says through Isaiah the prophet, "I'm going to create a new atmosphere and a new way, or a new way for the nations." He also says, "The former will not be remembered."

We won't even remember what life under the curse of the fall was like. That time won't matter to us, because we'll have glorified bodies, the same as Jesus has right now, and we'll be ruling with Jesus. But the folks in natural human bodies will get to experience the reversal of the fall.

But be ye glad and rejoice forever in that which I create: for, behold, I create Jerusalem a rejoicing, and her people a joy. And I will rejoice in Jerusalem, and joy in my people: and the voice of weeping shall be no more heard in her, nor the voice of crying.

Isaiah 65:18-19

There is no sadness or sorrow, grief or worry. All of these things are components of evil, remember? The curse actually came from eating the fruit of the tree of the knowledge of good and evil. Adam and Eve only knew what was good before eating the fruit salad of death. Suddenly, they had intimate knowledge of evil, which is made of those fifteen components: adversity, affliction, calamity, displeasure, distress (**WORRY**), exceeding great grief, harm, heaviness, hurt, ill favor (when somebody doesn't like you), misery, sadness, sorrow, trouble, and wrong.

There shall be no more thence an infant of days, nor an old man that hath not filled his days: for the child shall die an hundred years old; but the sinner being an hundred years old shall be accursed.

Isaiah 65:20

Let me untangle the King James for you. It says that if you are an infant, you're not going to die. If somebody a hundred years old dies, people will say, "Wow! That kid died young." The way we think now when a young child dies in a car wreck is how people will think during that time when someone dies at a hundred years old. And Isaiah says that an old man will fill out all of his days with a long life. The very next phrase says that the sinner being accursed shall die of a hundred years. So some remnants of the curse and sin are still going to be on the planet. People will marry and have children, and the children will have freewill. And apparently some of them won't choose Jesus.

And they shall build houses, and inhabit them; and they shall plant vineyards, and eat the fruit of them. They shall not build, and another inhabit; they shall not plant, and another eat: <u>for as the days of a tree are the days of my people</u>, and mine elect shall long enjoy the work of their hands.

Isaiah 65:21-22

(emphasis mine)

Here's a clue to how long those people who choose Jesus will live. How long do trees live? They live a long time. I know of some oak trees that are four hundred years old. I've been out to California to see the redwood forest, and those trees are a thousand years old and more. God's folks are going to live a really long natural life during the thousand year reign of Jesus.

They shall not labour in vain, nor bring forth for trouble; for they are the seed of the blessed of the LORD, and their offspring with them.

Isaiah 65:23

Here we see that people will be marrying and having babies and grand babies and great-grand babies. We won't bear children anymore, because we will be in our glorified bodies, but those who live through the tribulation and Armageddon will still have their natural earthly bodies. Why can their bodies live so long? Because the curse that went into the ground at the fall of man is lifted, the bodies which came from the ground can last a whole lot longer. The curse going into the ground was a really big deal.

And it shall come to pass, that before they call, I will answer; and while they are yet speaking, I will hear.

Isaiah 65:24

For this promise to happen for us right now would be great, that I wouldn't even have to pray. God would just show up with my answer, my financial miracle, or my healing, and whatever I needed would just show up before I even asked Him. We're not at that time yet. We still have to fight the good fight of faith, but this promise will happen during the millennial reign, when the curse of the fall is abated.

The wolf and the lamb shall feed together, and the lion shall eat straw like the bullock: and dust shall be the serpent's meat. They shall not hurt nor destroy in all my holy mountain, saith the LORD.

Isaiah 65:25

Interestingly, the same language used in the previous passage appears here again, cementing the time frame that Isaiah is speaking about in both Scriptures. Are you getting a picture of what the reversal of the curse of the fall is going to look like? Let's look at one more passage. I want to drive home what it's going to look like. This final Scripture takes place after the millennial (or thousand year) reign of Jesus, after the great white throne judgment and after God moves His throne and New Jerusalem from heaven to earth.

And he shewed me a pure river of water of life, clear as crystal, proceeding out of the throne of God and of the Lamb. In the midst of the street of it, and on either side of the river, was there the tree of life, which bare twelve manner of fruits, and yielded her fruit every month: and the leaves of the tree were for the healing of the nations. And there shall be no more curse: but the throne of God

and of the Lamb shall be in it; and his servants shall serve him.

Revelation 22:1-3

(emphasis mine)

The reason I'm reading this Scripture is that it states plain as day, "And there shall be no more curse." The other passages didn't state specifically the curse. This verse says unequivocally that the curse is no more. It's gone, completely eradicated. Jesus reverses the curse of the fall forever.

And they shall see his face; and his name shall be in their foreheads. And there shall be no night there; and they need no candle, neither light of the sun; for the Lord God giveth them light: and they shall reign for ever and ever.

Revelation 22:4-5

Doesn't it sound wonderful? What about right now, where we're all living? The apostle Paul gives us a situation report of our current state after

Jesus came, died, and rose again. We're living in between during what is known as the church age or dispensation of grace, fancy terms for "what's going on right now".

[But what of that?] For I consider that the sufferings of this present time (this present life) are not worth being compared with the glory that is about to be revealed to us and in us and for us and conferred on us!

Romans 8:18 (AMP)

The sufferings of this present time are that we are dealing with the curse of the fall. That's what sufferings Paul is talking about here, all the bad stuff in life, our bodies degenerating, resistance to work, nature competing with us. Aches and pains? Sure. We have to deal with the curse. Now, I'll tell you in a minute or two how Jesus made a way for us to get over these things so that victory is available for us to have, but we can't get around having to deal with the curse at present. That curse is why bad things happen to good people and bad alike. God didn't let it happen. Adam chose the curse, and he screwed us all up.

> **For [even the whole] creation (all nature) waits expectantly and longs earnestly for God's sons to be made known [waits for the revealing, the disclosing of their sonship]. For the creation (nature) was subjected to frailty (to futility, condemned to frustration), not because of some intentional fault on its part, but <u>by the will of him who so subjected it.</u>**
>
> **Romans 8:19-20**
>
> **(AMP, emphasis mine)**

Nature was not a willing participant in the curse of the fall. Adam's freewill choice to turn it over to Satan was what subjected it to the curse. Adam subjected all of nature to this frustrated state, this futility, and the earth and all of creation can't wait until it's fixed and operating the way God created it to function.

[Yet] with the hope that nature (creation) itself will be set free from its bondage to decay and corruption [and gain an entrance] into the glorious freedom of God's children.

Romans 8:20-21 (AMP)

We just read what will happen when nature and the earth are set free, in both Isaiah and Revelation. Nature is longing for the day when the curse is lifted.

We know that the whole creation [of irrational creatures] has been moaning together in the pains of labor until now.

Romans 8:22 (AMP)

When a woman goes into childbirth and transition labor, the intensity and pain overcome her in waves. The earth is going through that kind of labor right now. We see an increase in volcanoes erupting recently; another great earthquake ruins a city every other day, it seems. We see more tsunamis recently. The earth is going into transition labor. As we get closer to the end times, more and more of this kind of thing is going to occur. Jesus told us this increase would happen, and we're seeing it on the news every day and night. Nature is saying, "I am sick of this curse," and it cannot wait until Jesus comes back and redeems it from Satan and his cursed rule and reign.

And not only the creation, but we ourselves too, who have and enjoy the firstfruits of the [Holy] Spirit [a foretaste of the blissful things to come] groan inwardly as we wait for the redemption of our bodies [from sensuality and the grave, which will reveal] our adoption (our manifestation as God's sons).

Romans 8:23 (AMP)

I don't know about y'all, but I long for the day when I don't have to cut the grass or weed the flower beds. I long for the day that I don't have to change the oil in the car or deal with the brakes wearing out. I long for the day when the plumbing doesn't leak and the roof doesn't need repair after a thunderstorm. I long for the day when I don't have deal with hangnails or stubbed toes. I long for the day that I don't have to fight off headaches. I look forward to the day when there isn't any junk. Why do I long for that day? I got a foretaste of it on the inside of me when I believed on Jesus and entered the covenant.

In the first chapter of this book, we talked about living on God's Ponderosa. If you live inside the boundaries of the covenant on God's Ponderosa, inside the guidance of the Word, then you can literally have heaven on earth. God has made a way for us to experience heaven right now during this natural life. Does having heaven on earth mean that you won't suffer bad things? No, but what God does is give us the opportunity to have victory. An opportunity, I say, because you don't have to overcome, you don't have to be victorious. You get to win, if you want, but you don't have to have victory. Sadly, most Christians don't have victory.

The Curse of the Law

God provided a way for us to come back from the dark side, and here it is.

Christ hath redeemed us from the curse of the law, being made a curse for us: for it is written, Cursed is every one that hangeth on a tree.

Galatians 3:13

Do you remember step nine of the covenant ritual? Plant a tree, and sprinkle blood on it, which is what Jesus did on the cross. He was on the cross, God's covenant tree. God sprinkled Jesus' blood on it, and Jesus said, "It is finished." When Jesus died, He reversed or redeemed us from the curse of the law, reversing the effects of the dark side. He provided a way for us to have victory in this life, right now.

Warning: this next section is going to get kind of creepy, because we're going to take a trip to the dark side so that we can see exactly what we're up against. Once you know what the dark side is, I'll show you how He made a way back from it. Step seven of the covenant, the reciting of the terms of the covenant, also includes the consequences of violating the covenant. I'm not going to read through all the consequences because they get really, really creepy, down to like, eating your kids. We're not going to read that part, because hopefully we will never, ever get to that place in life.

Before we start, I want to put us in remembrance of the meaning of the word "blessing". In the Hebrew it means two things: (1) God kneeling down, literally kneeling down, and giving you a gift, and (2) the cultural meaning of consistently lucky success. "Cursing" is the opposite of blessing; so what we have is God standing up and not giving the gift. He's not kneeling down anymore handing us a gift. He's standing up. Also, we become consistently unlucky failures. Everywhere you see the word curse or cursing, think consistently unlucky failure. God can't kneel down and give you the gift anymore, because when you try to keep the law, you walk away from where He was kneeling; so God stands back up.

> **But if you will not obey the voice of the Lord your God, being watchful to do all His commandments and His statutes which I command you this day, then all these curses shall come upon you and overtake you.**
>
> **Deuteronomy 28:15 (AMP)**

Commandments are spoken, and statutes are written. If you are honest, you know you can't keep all of God's written words or all of His spoken words to you. If you try and fail, you are under the curse of the law. You must believe that what Jesus did is enough and take up His new command- ment, or all of these curses (consistently unlucky failures) will hunt you down and take you out.

> **Cursed shall you be in the city and cursed shall you be in the field.**
>
> **Deuteronomy 28:16 (AMP)**

You will be a consistently unlucky failure in the city or in the country.

Cursed shall be your basket and your kneading trough.
Deuteronomy 28:17 (AMP)

My basket and my kneading trough are my pantry, my fridge, and my freezer. If those were all consistently unlucky failures, they would always be empty.

Cursed shall be the fruit of your body, of your land, of the increase of your cattle and the young of your sheep.
Deuteronomy 28:18 (AMP)

Your children will be consistently unlucky failures. This curse alone makes me want to dump all the religious baggage that comes with keeping the law, just to save my kids from being consistently unlucky failures. I've seen so many "preacher's kids" (PKs) become such failures

because of their parents' intense effort to keep
the law and religious tradition.

**Cursed shall you be when you come in
and cursed shall you be when you go out.
The <u>Lord shall send</u> you curses, confusion, and rebuke <u>in every enterprise to
which you set your hand</u>, until you are
destroyed, perishing quickly because of
the evil of your doings by which you have
forsaken me [Moses and God as one].**

Deuteronomy 28:19-20

(AMP, emphasis mine)

The Hebrew for the phrase "the Lord shall
send" is actually permissive. Literally it says, "The
Lord will let depart unto you". He didn't send the
curses, but when you try to keep the law, what
you are saying is, "Jesus, I got this. What You did
wasn't enough; I have to keep God's law," and you
get up and walk away from Him while He was
kneeling down and handing you the gift. He says,
"All right, Andrew, go ahead." God is a gentleman;

you can walk away from Him any time you want to. And you trying to keep the Ten Commandments bring serious consequences: curses, consistently unlucky failures, confusion, and rebuke in every enterprise which you set your hand to, in whatever your job is, whatever business venture you undertake, even your hobbies. Do you like scuba diving? Forget about it. You try to keep the law, and even scuba diving will be a curse, haunted with consistently unlucky failure.

> **The Lord will make the pestilence cling to you until He has consumed you from the land into which you go to possess. The Lord will smite you with consumption, with fever and inflammation, fiery heat, sword and drought, blasting and mildew; they shall pursue you until you perish.**
>
> **Deuteronomy 28:21-22 (AMP)**

This stuff is going to hunt you down and eventually kill you. The curse of the fall is general; everyone on the planet feels its effects. When you enter into covenant with God and accept that what Jesus did was enough and then you walk away from the cross by trying to fulfill the law yourself, you are saying to God, "Jesus didn't do enough; I have to do good and shun bad in order to get the job done. Thanks, Jesus, but I've got this."

When you reject Him in pride, you have invited worse than the curse of the fall, because the curse of the law is specific. It will go after you specifically, hunt you down, and take you out. You would have been better off if you had never entered into the covenant in the first place, if you are just going to walk away from Jesus' sacrifice and take matters into your own hands. Keeping the law is the epitome of pride; you are becoming your own savior. The curse that comes with trying to keep the law hunts down specific people.

The Lord will smite you with the boils of Egypt and the tumors, the scurvy and the itch, from which you cannot be healed.
Deuteronomy 28:27 (AMP)

Imagine athlete's foot without a cure, no Desenex, no Gold Bond Medicated Powder, no cortisone for your rashes. Ouch.

The Lord will smite you with madness and blindness and dismay of [mind and] heart. And you shall grope at noonday as the blind grope in darkness. And <u>you shall not prosper in your ways</u>; and you shall be only oppressed and robbed continually, and there shall be no one to save you.

Deuteronomy 28:28-29

(AMP, emphasis mine)

You will only be oppressed or depressed, and robbed from continually, and there will be no one to save you, not family, not friends, not God. Imagine for a minute what it would be like to be ripped off everywhere you turn. The gas pump you pick is full of water and now so is your car. The cashier gives you back the wrong change, shorting you twenty bucks, and you don't notice it until it's too late. The bank loses your deposit, and your paycheck is put into someone else's account so that all your checks bounce. The water meter on your house is clicking away three gallons for every one gallon you use, and on and on and on.

And you shall become an amazement, a proverb, and a byword among all the peoples to which the Lord will lead you.
Deuteronomy 28:37 (AMP)

That word "amazement": I studied its root meaning in the Hebrew. It's a very technical term that means "carnie sideshow freak". Folks will say, "Look at that sideshow freak over there." You will be "an amazement" to people; they will shake their heads and think, "Why would I want to serve that person's God? I've got enough problems without being like him."

It also says you will be a proverb, and it doesn't mean a good proverb. Do you remember Jim Jones? He went to French Guyana and took his church with him in the 1970s, and they committed mass suicide by drinking cyanide-laced Kool Aid. What's the proverb now, forty years later? "Don't drink the Kool Aid" or "You've been drinking the Kool Aid". Those proverbs are all over the place, including the news broadcasts.

Further, the passage says that you will become a byword, and that means a word used to taunt or mock. You've heard people say, "He pulled a Homer Simpson". Folks will call your name and associate it with however stupid your actions are. You will be a byword.

You shall carry much seed out into the field and shall gather little in, for the locust shall consume it.

Deuteronomy 28:38 (AMP)

I have been brought up in church my entire life and taught to give. I used to give a lot but get only a little back, plant a lot of seed but not get a whole lot back in my harvest. Have you ever had that experience? You give a lot but receive back a little? I don't just mean money. Consider your love or help that you give to others. Here's an example: For years, Kimmi and I helped people move. We helped a lot of people move, packing the kitchen, loading the furniture, unpacking the kitchen, and setting up the beds at the new place. When the time came for us to move, I was standing there alone with my wife and a truck, and don't ever try to move furniture with your wife. That's a recipe for a domestic waiting to happen. *Why, Andrew? Do you blame the people you helped that they didn't help you?* No, the curse of the law was working in my life. I have been one of those guys from my youth keeping all the commandments, like the rich young ruler. The more I would work at keeping the law, the more negative things happened in my life. For the longest time, I couldn't figure out why. Finally, I just asked the Holy Spirit to show me what was going on. I wish someone had taught me stuff when I was younger; I could have avoided years of junk.

You shall plant vineyards and dress them but shall neither drink of the wine

nor gather the grapes, for the worm shall eat them.

Deuteronomy 28:39 (AMP)

We don't plant a lot of vineyards nowadays, but agriculture was a major industry during this time period. Let me bring the picture around to our culture. Have you ever, during your career or at your job, put a lot of effort into a project, and then someone else came along and received all the credit for your good work? Have you ever been an exemplary employee, always on time, reliable, giving the maximum effort, but then someone else gets the promotion or the pay raise? That snub is the curse of the law working in your life. We're just reading the Bible. Does this stuff happen to good Christian folks? It happens every day to good Christian folks, and the harder you try to keep all the law, the worse the curse is in your life.

The transient (stranger) among you shall mount up higher and higher above you, and you shall come down lower and

lower. He shall lend to you, but you shall not lend to him; he shall be the head, and you shall be the tail.

Deuteronomy 28:43-44 (AMP)

Our nation was built on Judeo-Christian values, which is code for the Ten Commandments. Have you ever heard that statement before? Our churches, regardless of denomination, base all their tenets on doing the Ten Commandments. No wonder a stranger (i.e. China) owns us. The United States is quickly becoming the tail and not the head. Maybe you have experienced this loss on a personal level.

You may know someone, not you, of course, who has a mountain of debt. Maybe he was in debt in the past and paid it off and then went back into debt. Does he have a mortgage on the house? Credit card debt? Owe a truck or car payment? These things are all part of the curse of the law. How can we possibly get out of it? Keep on reading.

All these curses shall come upon you and shall pursue you and overtake you till you are destroyed, because you do not obey the voice of the Lord your God, to keep His commandments and His statutes which He commanded you.

Deuteronomy 28:45 (AMP)

You must rely on the work of Jesus; you CANNOT keep all God's spoken Words or all of His written Words. Remember, commandments are spoken, and statues are written. How could you possibly keep all His statues unless you knew them all first? The Pharisees would memorize the law (the first five books of the Old Testament). You can't keep what you don't know. Without the work of Jesus and the covenant, all the curses, consistently unlucky failures, will pursue you and overtake you until you are eventually destroyed. Please stop trying to "be a good Christian" doing your checklists.

Then the Lord will bring upon you and your descendants extraordinary strokes and blows, great plagues of long continuance, and grievous sicknesses of long duration.

Deuteronomy 28:59 (AMP)

One of my relatives who was forty-seven years old, was out driving on the highway recently when he was struck down with a stroke. His oldest child was about to graduate high school, the day after the attack. Am I saying that this tragedy was the curse of the law? Well, he was born again, and I'm just reading the Bible. Christians experience bad things (AIDS, cancer, heart attacks, etc.) because of both the curse of the fall and the curse of the law, if they try to keep the law. Yes, we have to deal with junk, but we should have victory over all of it. Why don't we? I'm going to answer a lot of questions as to why Christians don't experience victory every single time something bad happens; just keep reading.

Moreover, He will bring upon you all the diseases of Egypt of which you were afraid, and they shall cling to you. Also every sickness and every affliction which is not written in this Book of the Law the Lord will bring upon you until you are destroyed. Your life shall hang in doubt before you; day and night you shall be worried, and have no assurance of your life. In the morning you shall say, <u>Would that it were evening!</u> and at evening you shall say, <u>Would that it were morning!</u>— because of the anxiety and dread of your [minds and] hearts and the sights which you shall see with your [own] eyes.

Deuteronomy 28:60-67

(AMP, emphasis mine)

Day and night, you will be worried or anxious. Anybody ever worry? Right now in the United States, we have no assurance of life. Watch the evening news or read the headlines on Yahoo about murders, earthquakes, fires, floods, tsunamis, terrorism, healthcare reform, national debt, and on and on and on. Why is everyone worried about Medicare and Social Security going bankrupt? Why do we fret over our IRAs and 401Ks? Why is health insurance such a big issue? People want assurance in this life, and they don't have it. Christians worry more than anybody else I know. I would rather have an unbeliever as a neighbor than a religious Christian.

In the evening you wish it were morning. In the morning you wish it were evening. Have you ever found yourself wishing away the days, the nights, the weeks, the months, or the years until retirement? This wishing away of life is the dark side.

I can sum up the dark side in three words. Under the curse of the law, you will be in debt, and your pantry will be empty. Every enterprise you attempt will fail. Word number one: **Poverty**. You will be an amazement, a sideshow freak. You will become a proverb, like Jim Jones and the Kool Aid. You will become a byword, like Homer Simpson. Word number two: **Dishonor**. You will suffer from sicknesses and diseases and illnesses and plagues of long duration that can't be healed until you are destroyed. Word number three: **Death**.

Wait a minute, what were the three words that summed up the covenant? Riches, honor, and life: those words are the exact opposite of the three words that sum up the dark side, the curse of the law. Say this out loud so you can hear it with your own ears, "Jesus reversed the curse of the law in my life." Say it again, "Jesus reversed the curse of the law in my life." Your Redeemer has reversed anything that falls under poverty (or lack), dishonor, or death in your life. People ask me all the time, "That sounds nice, Andrew, but why don't I see riches, honor, and life happening for me?"

Before I get into the whys and why nots, let me tell you about another news story I saw this past week, and look at the way our society is going. Somebody once again sued to have the Ten Commandments taken out of a public park. Do you remember that state Supreme Court justice from Alabama? That man put his money where his mouth was. He was the highest judge in that state, and he lost his job because he fought for what he believed: keeping the Ten Commandments on a monument inside of the court house.

I believe I already know the answer to this question, but don't you think the Ten Commandments are a good thing to have posted inside a court house? Wouldn't you agree with this statement? The basic foundation of anyone acting right as a Christian would be due to the Ten Commandments; it's the Christian Code or Credo. Does anybody who is a Christian out there seek to violate the Ten Commandments? If you're trying to be a good Christian, you are trying to keep the Ten Commandments, aren't you? Keeping them is what we as Christians do, isn't it? We try, at least, the very least, to keep the Ten Commandments.

Hold on, we're talking about why Christians don't experience riches, honor, and life, the reversal of the curse of the law. Why don't all sick Christians get healed? Why are so many Christians poor and can barely feed their families? Why do many Christian marriages fail and end in divorce? *(WARNING: The following teaching ill challenge your religious upbringing!)*

The Reason Why Christians
Don't Experience Riches, Honor, and Life

I'm going to tell you why Christians don't experience the reversal of the dark side or the curse of the law. Buckle up! This next paragraph is going to blow your mind and start you on the path to riches, honor, and life. Meditate on this next verse, mull it over, and you will begin to eradicate the effects of the dark side in your life. We Christians are trying so very hard to keep the Ten Commandments so that God will be pleased with us. Most of us can keep the Ten Commandments pretty well, but the law starts with the Ten Commandments in Exodus 20 and doesn't finish until the end of Deuteronomy, with Leviticus and Numbers in between. To keep the law, you have to do everything between Exodus 20 and Deuteronomy 34.

For <u>as many as are of the works of the law are under the curse</u>: for it is written, Cursed is every one that continueth not

in all things **which are written in the book of the law to do them.**

Galatians 3:10,

emphasis mine

Read that verse again. Now read it again. The harder you work at keeping the Ten Commandments, the worse the curse will appear in your life. Jesus redeemed us from the curse of the law, and then we put ourselves right back under it. I don't blame you; I blame the ministers, pastors, and priests of all denominations for this suffering. They have been putting the people of God under the curse, nullifying everything Jesus did, and they have been doing it since 325 AD when Constantine, Emperor of Rome, took over the church.

The second half of verse 10 states that a person is cursed if he doesn't continue in all things written in the book of the law to do them. Surely I don't have to convince you that you aren't doing everything written in the law from Exodus 20 to Deuteronomy 34, do I? Not only are you not doing everything, you **CANNOT** do everything. That's right: **CANNOT**; keeping the law during the church age is impossible.

I'm going to cite just one small example of the law that none of us is keeping or can keep.

> **For the Pharisees, and all the Jews, except they wash their hands oft, eat not, holding the tradition of the elders. And when they come from the market, except they wash, they eat not. And many other things there be, which they have received to hold, as the washing of cups, and pots, brasen vessels, and of tables.**
>
> **Mark 7:3-4**

The law commanded its keepers to wash their hands. They would keep this part of the law in a ceremonial washing bowl, called a mikvah. When they would go out to the marketplace, before they would eat, they would wash in the mikvah, in order to keep the law. Until you washed, you were what the law called "unclean". The Pharisees were very upset that Jesus' disciples weren't washing their hands, thus violating the law.

If he touch the uncleanness of man, whatsoever uncleanness it be that a man shall be defiled withal, and it be hid from him; when he knoweth of it, then he shall be guilty.

Leviticus 5:3

If you haven't washed in a mikvah before your last meal, you haven't kept the law and are under the curse. If you didn't know this duty before, I'm telling you now, and now you are guilty if you don't keep this part of the law along with the Ten Commandments.

Have you ever used a public restroom? Did you use a mikvah after you were finished? Have you ever shaken hands with someone that has not used a mikvah? Even if you do and then you shake hands with someone who doesn't, you are unclean. If you don't use a mikvah and you shake my hand, you are causing me to sin and become unclean. Thanks a lot.

Wait, you didn't know. That's not fair. You didn't know that the person who shook your hand didn't use a mikvah. God's is fair and just; so He made a solution to the problem that you just didn't know (even though now you do).

If a soul commit a trespass, and sin through ignorance, in the holy things of the LORD; then he shall bring for his trespass unto the LORD a ram <u>without blemish</u> out of the flocks, with thy estimation by shekels of silver, after the shekel of the sanctuary, for a trespass offering.

Leviticus 5:15

(emphasis mine)

God is saying, "Don't bring me a cheap sheep. You must go out and buy a good sheep. Then you have to take it to the priest, and the priest must sacrifice the good sheep on the altar. Once that happens, you will be clean again, and your sin of shaking hands with someone after they went to the public restroom and didn't wash in a mikvah will be pushed back."

Have you ever taken a cheap sheep over to Jerusalem – I mean a good sheep, not a cheap sheep, to the priest at the Temple in order to sacrifice it to keep the law? Wait a minute; they don't do animal sacrifices anymore at the Temple. What? There isn't even a Temple; an Islamic shrine is there now?

Don't you see that we don't even have a way to keep the law today? We CANNOT follow the law; keeping it isn't even possible. Even the Orthodox Jews can't keep the law. Oh, they try to keep all that they can, but without an altar and animal sacrifice, their task is impossible. If you realize that this obstacle is valid, then why do you try to keep the Ten Commandments? We put ourselves under the law and under the curse. This effort is the number one reason why Christians don't have victory and don't experience the covenant benefits of riches, honor, and life. We continue to put ourselves on the dark side of the law and experience poverty, dishonor, and death.

Most us will never end up eating our kids because of famine or deal with total poverty, but most of us aren't ever going to experience riches, honor, and life, either. We're in the middle. The spiritual middle class is the biggest lie from hell that ever was, right after religion. Why? If you are in the spiritual middle class, you aren't desperate enough to get on board with the covenant totally and actually (oh no, not that!) believe God and His Word. We in the middle class are too comfortable living life between the forty-yard lines to risk what little we have for the covenant. And remember, the covenant is reciprocal; God can only give to you at the level that you give to Him. So you'll never get riches by tithing (ten percent). If you give God ten percent, He can legally give to you just ten percent.

Jesus said in Revelation that He would rather us be hot or cold, but being lukewarm makes Him sick. The second reason Christians don't experience riches, honor, and life is that we're just fine living in the middle, lukewarm. We are so afraid that God won't really take care of us that we don't want to get too crazy with this "God stuff". *See, the Ten Commandments are reasonable, Andrew. I am a good, law-abiding citizen. I don't experience the high side, but I'm also not experiencing the lowest of the low side. Let's just be happy with where we are. Being a law abiding citizen is where I'm comfortable with my faith.*

The level that we do the law is level that we stay under the curse. The harder you work at your good citizen checklist, the bigger the curse looms in your life. Ever notice how some nonbelievers seem "blessed" and have consistently lucky success? They aren't even in the covenant. You work hard at doing all the right things, but nothing seems to go your way.

But that no man is justified by the law in the sight of God, it is evident: for, The just shall live by faith. And the law is not of faith: but, The man that doeth them shall live in them.

Galatians 3:11-12

The man that does the law shall live in it. And if you live in the law, you live under the curse of it. So you have to deal with two curses, the curse of the fall and the curse of the law. Double whammy! You must dump the Ten Commandments if you want to have victory in life. *Andrew, have you lost your mind?* No, I have not, but who cares what I say? I don't care what any man, woman, or child says or thinks; I just want to know what God says and thinks and then adopt that thinking. Let's see what Jesus says.

A <u>new commandment</u> I give unto you, that ye love one another; as I have loved you, that ye also love one another.

John 13:34

(emphasis mine)

A what? Jesus Himself gives us a <u>new commandment</u>. He says the word "love" three times in this short commandment. Love one another; the way I love you is how you are to love one another. Get out from under the Ten Commandments. Get out from under the law. Get out from under the curse. Now get under this new commandment: walk in love.

We just read that the law is not of faith and the just shall live by faith. Now you're telling me to live by love, Andrew? This verse is one of my favorites in the Bible.

For in Jesus Christ neither circumcision availeth any thing, nor uncircumcision; but faith which worketh by love.

Galatians 5:6

The people in the church at Galatia were told that, in order to be born again, they had to keep the law and do step number five of the covenant ritual, which was to be circumcised. Paul is saying that neither keeping the law nor not keeping the law brings any benefit when you have believed on Jesus.

Most Christians end up in these two ditches. First they try really hard to keep the law, an effort which brings them no benefit. When that effort begins to wear them out, as eventually happens to everyone trying to keep the law, they see no benefit and go into the other ditch of doing nothing. Doing nothing, uncircumcision, brings no benefit either, and after awhile guilt sets in. Then most folks will go back to the first ditch of trying to keep the law. This entire cycle usually happens every week. Sunday we're in the law ditch, and by mid-week, we're in the other ditch. And then we jerk the wheel back to keeping the law on the following Sunday.

So what are we to do? The opposite of keeping the law is faith, believing that what Jesus did was enough for you to measure up with God. Paul tells us that faith works by means of love. Jesus said, "A new commandment I give unto you, Love one another the way I have loved you." Dump the law. Dump the Ten Commandments. Dump the curse of the law, and take up the new commandment of loving one another.

The first time I taught this doctrine, many people, my wife included, said, "Surely you aren't saying that the Ten Commandments are bad?"

No, but they weren't written to you; they were written to the physical bloodline of Abraham until the Seed, Christ came. Jesus perfected us forever with His sacrifice. If you have accepted Jesus' sacrifice, when God looks at you, He sees you as completely perfect, forever.

By the which will we are sanctified through the offering of the body of Jesus Christ once for all ...for by one offering he hath perfected for ever them that are sanctified.

Hebrews 10:10, 14

Two More Reasons Why Christians Don't Experience Riches, Honor, and Life

Christians don't experience the reversal of the curse of the law for two more reasons. I'm reminded of a story.

Once upon a time, there was a missionary couple who were brought up during the Depression, and they had no children. They were mainline denominational missionaries (which denomination doesn't matter). They were very hard-working folks. They never owned a house, and never had a brand new car. They wore secondhand clothing and got their groceries from the food pantry at various supporting churches.

They faithfully worked and worked for many years. Finally, in the late 70s, before *The Love Boat* came out and was really big, at the time before cruises were for mainline society, they received a four day and three night cruise from an anonymous benefactor. Prior to the couple going on the cruise, they scrimped and saved and managed to put together fifty bucks for their budget for one fabulous meal. They went to the church food pantry and stocked up on Vienna sausages, saltine crackers, and peanut butter for the rest of the trip. They packed the food in their luggage and took their collapsible folding travel cups, to drink water in their cabin with their snack crackers.

When the couple arrived on board, everything they saw was fantastic and wonderful, like nothing they had ever experienced. They were really enjoying themselves, but at mealtimes, they would go to their cabin and eat the crackers and drink water. They saved their fifty bucks to eat one dinner onboard on the last night of the cruise so that they could make a memory together.

The big night finally arrived. They knew that fifty bucks wouldn't go far in such a fancy restaurant; so they were going to split one entrée and order water to drink. They found their way to one of the ship's restaurants and were seated. Looking at the menu, they noticed no prices listed next to the selections. The couple shyly beckoned the waiter over and said, "We're embarrassed. We're missionaries, and we only have fifty dollars. Which entrée can we get? The menu doesn't list any prices, and we want to split a dish with the fifty dollars. We also want to leave you a tip; so keep that in mind as well."

Astonished, the waiter asked, "What have you been eating the entire cruise?"

"Well," said the husband, "We've been eating peanut butter crackers in our cabin and some others snack crackers. We only have fifty dollars to spend tonight; could you please tell us which entrée we could split?"

The waiter was completed astounded, "The food is part of your ticket; it's included in your fare. We have six restaurants onboard, and three of them are open twenty-four hours a day. You could have eaten at any or all of them the entire trip. It's all part of the ticket."

The couple didn't experience all that the cruise included because they didn't know what belonged to them. They just didn't know. They were out of their element, and nobody told them until the end. This ignorance is one of the saddest reasons why Christians don't experience the reversal of the curse of the law in their lives. They simply don't know what belongs to them. They don't know the benefits of the covenant; they don't know about the covenant.

My people are destroyed for lack of knowledge: because thou hast rejected knowledge, I will also reject thee.

Hosea 4:6

God's people are destroyed because they just don't know what belongs to them or how to get it. The blame for this lack of knowledge falls squarely on the ministers' shoulders for the past seventeen hundred years.

God states another reason Christians don't experience riches, honor, and life in the second half of the verse. You do have a choice. Do you reject the knowledge of what God provided for you in the covenant? Do you believe riches, honor, and life belong to you? Sadly, most Christians reject the knowledge because their life-long experience with the church and church people does not line up with riches, honor, and life. Most Christians and most ministers say, "That promise is not for today, brother. It ended when the last apostle died. The Bible only speaks of spiritual riches."

Such statements are very sad to me. Nowhere in the entire Bible will you find the term "spiritual riches". It's not even a concept in the Bible; remember, Proverbs speaks of "durable riches". The rejection of this knowledge brings a consequence. God says that, because you reject knowledge, I will also reject you. No wonder bad things happen to Christians.

Most of Christianity today is living in this state, rejecting what Jesus did and trying to keep the law. Turn on any Christian radio station, any talk radio, any conservative radio, and you'll hear all about the commandments and how the country is going to hell in a hand basket. The ACLU is trying to deny our founding fathers' Judeo-Christian values. Who cares? We just do what we're supposed to do; we're no longer under the Ten Commandments. If we embraced loving one another the way Jesus loves us and embraced the knowledge of riches, honor, and life, we would be in the driver's seat, the position of honor.

Christians are weak, the laughing stock of the world. We have become an amazement and a byword. If we actually grabbed hold of the covenant, the ACLU would be coming to us for answers, and the country would be looking to the church for solutions to healthcare reform, debt reduction, and assurance of life. Sadly, the church is weak, always begging for money, in a constant uproar over violations of the Ten Commandments in society, and confusing politics with faith. We are the tail and not the head.

CHAPTER 4

The New Commandment

Those in covenant experienced a section of time, about fifteen hundred seventy years, when they were under the law. The law was pointing those in covenant towards the Seed, Christ.

> **But before faith came, we were kept under the law, shut up unto the faith which should afterwards be revealed. Wherefore the law was our schoolmaster to bring us unto Christ, that we might be justified by faith. But after that faith is come, we are no longer under a school-**

master. For ye are all the children of God by faith in Christ Jesus.

Galatians 3:23-26

This passage reminds me of that movie *Uncle Buck* with John Candy. It's a very funny movie about a crazy uncle who's taking care of his niece and nephew. Uncle Buck's six year old niece gets called into the principal's office, and Uncle Buck has to have a conference with the principal. The principal is an old hag, with a ginormous, hairy mole on her face. She states, "I have been an educator for exactly 32.3 years, and your niece is a bad egg." She goes on and on about the little girl not taking life and her studies seriously. Uncle Buck throws her a quarter and tells her to call a cab, go downtown, and have a rat gnaw that mole off her face.

I want you to see that mental picture in your head every time you read in the Bible or hear anyone speak about the law in church. Picture the old hag schoolmaster riding your case because you are not taking the performance of the good and bad checklists seriously enough. Paul paints the picture for us in this passage that the law was a schoolmaster, past tense, keeping those in covenant in line until Jesus could get here on the scene to redeem us.

Now, present tense, that we have faith in Christ, we are no longer under the old hag schoolmaster. We have graduated from school; we don't have to worry about chewing gum in class anymore. We are allowed to chew gum anytime and anywhere we please. You don't have to raise your hand and ask to go to the potty. You can just go to the potty whenever you need to go. You don't need a hall pass any longer, and you don't have to sweat the safety patrol or hall monitors giving you detention or demerits.

If you want to experience being redeemed from the curse of the law, if you want to experience riches, honor, and life, you must get out from under the schoolmaster. To have the schoolmaster telling you what can and cannot do was no fun. You will never experience all that God offers us in the covenant sitting in the classroom with a group of people sitting in class under the schoolmaster. As long as you sit under a minister that preaches the schoolmaster, as long as you stay with a group that keeps itself under the schoolmaster, as long as you try to keep the Ten Commandments, you will never experience all that Jesus paid for you to have in life.

Well, Andrew, what do I do then? What I think or say about it doesn't matter one little bit; I'm just a man. We need to find out what God thinks and says about what to do.

A new commandment I give unto you, that ye love one another; as I have loved you, that ye also love one another.

John 13:34

In order to fulfill this new commandment, the first thing we have to do is find out how Jesus loved us. If we are going to love one another the way Jesus loved us, we have to know exactly how He loved us. Jesus gives us a list of how He loved us. People have this image of Jesus as some hippy,

Birkenstock-wearing guru from the lost tribes of Vermont, with a burlap toga and a tie-dyed T-shirt with Indian art stapled to it. That image does NOT describe how Jesus is at all.

How Jesus Loves Us

As the Father hath loved me, so have I loved you: continue ye in my love. If ye keep my commandments, ye shall abide in my love; even as I have kept my Father's commandments, and abide in his love. <u>These things</u> have I spoken unto you, that my joy might remain in you, and that your joy might be full. This is my commandment, that ye love one another, as I have loved you. Greater love hath no man than this, that a man lay down his life for his friends. Ye are my friends, if ye do whatsoever I command you. Henceforth I call you not servants; for the servant knoweth not what his lord doeth: but I have called you

friends; for all things that I have heard of my Father I have made known unto you. Ye have not chosen me, but I have chosen you, and ordained you, that ye should go and bring forth fruit, and that your fruit should remain: that whatsoever ye shall ask of the Father in my name, he may give it you. These things I command you, that ye love one another.

John 15:9-17

(emphasis mine)

These things: Jesus red flags us twice by repeating "these things". What things? Jesus lists the tangible things that He does to show His love for us. Too many times when we read the Bible, trying to accomplish reading it through in one year, we end up breezing over very important truths. How many times have we read the words of Jesus and not sat down with the Holy Spirit to ask Him for understanding? We're going to go through this passage and look at those things Jesus gives us. Why? Jesus never tells us to do something without telling us how to do it. He gives us the new commandment and then tells how we can pull it off.

> **These things have I spoken unto you, that my joy might remain in you, and that your joy might be full.**
>
> **John 15:11**
>
> **(emphasis mine)**

The very first thing we must have in order to fulfill the new commandment, Jesus says, is His joy remaining in us so that our joy might be full. Where does the joy of the Lord come from, and how do we tap into it? If we need it, where and how can we get it?

The Joy of the Lord

Let's flash back to the time in Israel's history at the end of their seventy years of captivity in Babylon. To give you a point of reference, during this captivity Daniel was thrown into the lions' den, and those guys (Shadrach, Meshach, and Abednego) got tossed into the fiery furnace for not worshipping a statue of the Babylonian king. Jerusalem's wall was destroyed, as was the Temple.

A guy named Nehemiah got tapped by the king of Persia, who took down the Babylonians, to go back to his homeland and rebuild Jerusalem's wall, rebuild the city, and rebuild the Temple. Nehemiah packed his gear, grabbed a priest named Ezra, and headed off to start the rebuilding project. "Build it, and they will come": the strategy worked. As Nehemiah rebuilt, people came home from captivity and gathered in Jerusalem.

During the project, for the first time in seventy years, the congregation of covenant people gathered and heard the Bible publicly read. For the first time in seventy years, they were having church: we're talking about the joy of the Lord.

So they read in the book in the law of God distinctly, and gave the sense, and <u>caused them to understand</u> the reading. And Nehemiah, which is the Tirshatha,

and Ezra the priest the scribe, and the Levites that taught the people, said unto all the people, This day is holy unto the LORD your God; mourn not, nor weep. For all the people wept, when they heard the words of the law. Then he said unto them, Go your way, eat the fat, and drink the sweet, and send portions unto them for whom nothing is prepared: for this day is holy unto our LORD: neither be ye sorry; <u>for the joy of the LORD is your strength</u>. So the Levites stilled all the people, saying, Hold your peace, for the day is holy; neither be ye grieved. And all the people went their way to eat, and to drink, and to send portions, and to make great mirth, <u>because they had understood the words</u> that were declared unto them.

Nehemiah 8:8-12

(emphasis mine)

Jesus told us to be full of His joy and that His joy should remain in us as one of the "these things" list of instructions on fulfilling the new commandment. Verse 10 makes this statement, "for the joy of the LORD is your strength." Whose joy does this verse mean: your joy or the Lord's joy? It is the Lord's joy. Whose strength does it mean: your strength or the Lord's? It is your strength. According to the Scripture, God gets joy when His people are in a position of strength. When you do well in life and understand the covenant, you give your Father great joy. God had great joy that His covenant people were out of captivity, rebuilding their inheritance, and beginning to understand the covenant.

Notice that, as they came out of captivity and began to rebuild their lives, they were made to understand the covenant. They began to understand that riches, honor, and life were God's will for their lives. At first this truth caused them to weep and be sad. Why would good news like this make the people sad? I've seen this reaction over and over again as a pastor. When folks understand what belongs to them and then look at their lives, they don't see any way possible that they could ever enjoy riches, honor, and life. Most people then reject the truth of the covenant and go back to religion and the law.

Ezra, the priest, tells them to get happy and have a party. He tells them that God is thrilled that they finally understand that the covenant is about them being in a position of strength or honor. Was being a captive a position of strength or honor, or was it a position of weakness and dishonor? My prayer is that this book is doing for you what Ezra did for covenant people back then, causing you to understand the covenant and get the sense of it.

God is our Father. I, as a father, am filled with joy when my kids do well in life. All three of my kids are in martial arts. I can't tell you the joy I get when they are promoted to the next belt and I see them break boards. I see strength in them, and their strength gives me great joy. When they all three come home with excellent grades in school, I see strength, and their strength gives me great joy.

I have never, one time, felt joy when any of kids were fighting off sickness and fever. I have never, one time, felt joy when any of my kids fell down and skinned their knees. I have never, one time as a parent, felt joy when my kids couldn't understand a subject in school and were struggling to get it. Why do we think God is any different than we are? We are created in His image and likeness. Our Heavenly Father is filled with joy when we do well in life.

In order to love another the way He loves us, maybe we should be filled with joy when our fellow brothers and sisters in Christ do well in life instead of comparing ourselves with others and competing with others because "so and so is doing better than me". Not stealing from your brothers and sisters in Christ, not killing them, and not lying to them is easier than loving them. Taking up the new commandment and dumping the Ten Commandments is harder than it looks on the surface. You are not getting one over on God by dumping the law.

The new commandment is also not as hard as you think, either, People think that walking in love is just "love, peace, and turn the other cheek". But we live a real life in the real world. Walking in love is not letting people run roughshod all over you and others. Let's continue looking at the list of "these things" Jesus laid out for us in John 15.

Laying Down Your Life for Others

Greater love hath no man than this, that a man lay down his life for his friends.

John 15:13

That's great, Andrew. Jesus laid down His life for us, but how does that sacrifice pertain to us fulfilling the new commandment?

Hereby perceive we the love of God, because he laid down his life for us: and we ought to lay down our lives for the brethren.

1 John 3:16

Let's ask ourselves a few questions to help us understand what Jesus and John are saying. Do we all need to get whipped with a Roman scourge like He did? Do we all need to get nailed to a cross like He did? If we do, the sacrifice of Jesus was of no effect. So what are these verses of Scripture talking about? How do I lay down my life?

Right before the Romans arrested Jesus in the garden, He was praying, "Not my will Father, but yours be done." He wasn't praying, "Oh, God, whatever Your will is, let that be done." He knew what the Father's will was, no question about it, and His flesh didn't like it. Jesus prayed, "If there is any other way to do this, let's do that, but if not, I will make my will match up to yours, Father." He laid down His will for our sake. That example is what laying down your life for others means. You put your agenda for yourself on the back burner for others.

If Jesus had not laid down His will and gone with God's will, we would not have eternal life available to us. Mankind would have been doomed forever if He hadn't laid down His will for us. His will was to call down twelve legions of angels and lay waste to this planet of ungrateful pagan-piggies. I guarantee that the angels were up there waiting for the word to come swooping down to engage in battle. Any warrior knows that they were.

When we lay our lives down for one another, we fulfill the new commandment, which is simply being obedient enough to lay aside our own agendas for our lives and go help somebody else, somebody who would not get help if we didn't do what God asked us to do. If any other way is available, God will do His will another way. Remember, Jesus only proceeded after He found no other way. The key to this obedience is to know the Father's will and to know that there isn't any other way. I know some ministers who are so busy helping everybody that comes along that they neglect their own children. That neglect is NOT the Father's will.

To give a clearer picture of this "lay down your life" thing, I'd like to share a bit of my mother-in-law's life. She's an amazing woman. You know she is if her son-in-law is saying so. She exemplifies laying down one's life. In particular, she was a clear example a few years back when she decided to get a part-time job at the mall during the holiday season. At the time, she was the administrator for a very successful medical practice, a very busy, high-stress position, and she was quite successful (i.e. she didn't need a part-time job).

When she was over for dinner, she said, "You know, I think the Lord is telling me to get a part-time job at such and such shop at the mall for the holidays." I asked her if she was crazy; she didn't have time for that kind of nonsense. She wouldn't be able to spend time with the grandbabies, and her weekends would be gone, with no time to recover from the busy work week, etc.

She said, "No, I really think the Lord is telling me to get this job." She was obedient and laid down her life; she just didn't know why yet. Isn't that just like the Lord to leave out the details and whys? She worked for ten weeks straight without any days off. She was working all the time, and when she wasn't working one place, she was working some more at the other. The second job was only paying minimum wage, and driving there with the price of gas almost cost her money.

Soon, within a week or two, she saw that God loved someone at that shop who needed help. If Mom hadn't taken that job and laid down her agenda for the holiday season, that person would not have known that God loved her. She received help from heaven through my mother-in-law, in a big way. Did God have any other way to get help to this woman, whom He loved? Why didn't she just come to church? Well, friends, the sad truth is that church is the source of hurt in people's lives far more often than it is a source of help. As He has done with many others who have checked out of church, the Shepherd went after the one lost and hurting sheep. If Mom hadn't gone, who would have?

Well, one job isn't really a big deal, Andrew. God took two thousand years to find a man that would cut covenant with Him and not withhold his only son from Him. How many people died needing a Redeemer from the time Adam sinned until Abraham laid down his life for us? So the next time you're whining about why God is taking so long to help you, remember that the only way He can get help to you is through people. We are the body of Christ, His hands and feet here on planet earth. If you aren't getting help fast enough from heaven, chances are pretty high (one hundred percent) that somebody didn't lay down his agenda for you.

The next time God asks you to do something, remember that feeling so that you are quick to lay down your life and agenda for somebody else. Don't be the reason that someone doesn't get help. People don't get help instantly, because God has to work with and through people. I know how I am, and I don't always listen that well. I honestly don't know how He gets anything done here on the earth at all. If He asks something of us that we think will make us look stupid or crazy or just out of the norm for us, we don't want to do it. I wouldn't have taken that retail job: it was the holidays, I was tired, I had a family, I didn't speak well, (no wait, that was Moses, sorry). Thank God for my mother-in-law and folks like her, who willingly go out and lay their lives down for their brothers and sisters; they are a rare find.

We Are All Equals

Ye are my friends, if ye do whatsoever I command you. Henceforth I call you not servants; for the servant knoweth not what his lord doeth: but I have called you friends; for all things that I have heard of my Father I have made known unto you.

John 15:14-15

He calls us friends, not servants. He's not withholding anything from us. People have said that knowledge is power, and here is the Creator of the universe giving us the inside track. He's not holding back any information from us. He treats us as equals and peers. He pulls us up to His level, and He treats us like a peer, an equal with Him.

If anybody that ever walked the planet had the right to look down on others, Jesus would be that person. He is the only one ever to pull off life perfectly.

He doesn't look down on us, though. He lifts us up and puts us on a equal plane with Himself.

The Spirit itself beareth witness with our spirit, that we are the children of God: and if children, then heirs; heirs of God, and <u>joint-heirs with Christ</u>; if so be that we suffer with him, that we may be also glorified together.

Romans 8:16-17

(emphasis mine)

Jesus pulls us up. God looks at us and sees us the same as He sees Jesus. We're on an equal playing field with our Redeemer; we're the same in the Father's eyes. When I became a federal agent working to protect the highest levels of the US Senate and US House of Representatives, people were impressed. I was promoted to the position of Special Agent in Charge of Congresswoman Nancy Pelosi's security detail, and people would "ooh and ah" and be very impressed. They still are. But when I was pulling carts in the Sam's Wholesale Club parking lot, people weren't that impressed.

Whether you are the CEO of a Fortune 500 company, a plumber, a construction worker, a federal agent, a public office holder, a fast food worker, or a minister doesn't matter, for we are all joint-heirs with Christ. The Greek meaning of joint-heirs is co-equal heirs, co-equals with Jesus. If that position is true, and it is, then what you do is not who you are. Who you are, according to the Creator, is a co-equal heir with Jesus Christ. With that said, we need to be careful how we treat each other. He treats us as His equal, and you had better be very careful about treating His equals like you're better than they are. We aren't better than anybody, and we're not worse either. Some of you need to stand up straight, get your head up, start acting like an equal of Jesus, and stop believing that you don't measure up and that "so and so" is better or more spiritual than you are.

He Is Vouching For Us

That whatsoever ye shall ask of the Father in my name, he may give it you.

John 15:16

Most folks in church have skipped over this verse because they haven't experienced it. This statement of Jesus' is not a magic lamp to rub before you tell God your three wishes. What's going on here is that Jesus is vouching for us to the Father. What He does would be like a friend of my oldest son, Drew, coming up to me and saying, "Drew said I could borrow his bike." What's Drew's friend doing? He's asking Drew's father in Drew's name for what he wants.

As Drew's dad, I would naturally ask Drew, "Did you tell this guy he could borrow your bike?" I'm going to check with Drew that he knows the person making the request and that Drew vouches for him. Jesus is telling us that one of the ways He shows His love for us is that He vouches for us with the Father.

Who shall lay any thing to the charge of God's elect? It is God that justifieth. Who is he that condemneth? It is Christ that died, yea rather, that is risen again, who is even at the right hand of God, who also maketh intercession for us.

Romans 8:33-34

What is Jesus doing at the right hand of the Father? He is, at this very moment, making intercession for us. When you read intercession, what your brain tells you is that Jesus is praying for us. But He isn't. He's vouching for us; He is vouching for YOU to the Father, right now. He's saying to the Father, "Yes, I know him. I know her. That's one of my friends, and he can borrow my bike."

Jesus loves us so much that He spends His time standing at the right hand of the Father and vouching for us. What He does is intercession. Remember, the new commandment is to love one another the way He loves us. Maybe we should intercede for each other. How? What do we say? What difference would our intercession make? Should we just ask the Father to bless our brothers and sisters? How can we effectively intercede for each other?

In Ephesians, Paul reveals to us how he prays for us and how the Holy Spirit prays for us. He writes out the prayer the Holy Spirit prays, and I have been praying it over myself for years. My wife prays this prayer over our children and teaches them to pray it for themselves and others. As a pastor, I pray this prayer over those in my church. We pray it out loud every day and insert specific names as we pray it. If this prayer is good enough for Paul to pray for us and for the Holy Spirit to pray for us, maybe we should probably pray it for ourselves and others.

We have seen lives change after praying this prayer day in and day out. This prayer is like working out. You don't realize any results at first, but after about three to six months of daily praying this prayer, you'll suddenly see results in your own life and those for whom you have been praying it. This prayer is also what we pray for unbelievers.

I have written out the prayer as you would pray it for yourself. As you pray for others, just insert their names, change the tense from first person "me" to third person "him/her/them", and pray it out loud. Vocal prayer sounds weird, but you can't vouch for anyone silently. Jesus isn't silent when He's vouching for us.

I cease not to give thanks, making mention in my prayers; that You, the God of My Lord Jesus Christ, the Father of glory, may give unto me [say your own name] the spirit of wisdom, and revelation in the knowledge of You and Your Word: the eyes of my understanding being enlightened; that I may know and experience what is the hope of Your calling for me, and know and experience the riches of the glory of Your inheritance in the saints, for me. And that I may know and experience what is the exceeding greatness of Your power towards me, who believes, according to the working of

Your mighty power, which You wrought in Christ, when You raised him from the dead, and set Him at Your own right hand in the heavenly places, far above all principality, and power, and might, and dominion, and every name that is named, not only in this world, but also in that which is to come: and have put all things under His feet, and gave Him to be the head over all things to the church, which is His body, the fullness of Him that filleth all in all.

Ephesians 1:16-23

(emphasis mine)

For this cause I bow my knees unto the Father of my Lord Jesus Christ, of whom the whole family in heaven and earth is named, that <u>You would grant unto me,</u> according to the riches of Your glory, <u>to be strengthened with might by Your Spirit in my inner man;</u> that Christ may dwell in my heart by faith; that I, being

rooted and grounded in love, may be able to comprehend with all saints what is the breadth, and length, and depth, and height; and to know the love of Christ, which passes human knowledge, that I might be filled with all the fullness of God. Now unto Him that is able to do exceeding abundantly above that I ask or think, according to the power that works in me. Unto You be glory in the church by Christ Jesus throughout all ages, world without end. Amen.

Ephesians 3:14-21

(emphasis mine)

Jesus in Action

Jesus gave us a pretty good running start on fulfilling the new commandment by giving us His list of "these things" on how to love one another. But this great lesson is only theory, and I always want to see how biblical principles work in real life and real time. If we look at the very beginning of Jesus' ministry and the very end of it, He shows us how to walk in love in real life and real time. Jesus only had around three years in the ministry total. Nowadays, a lot of ministers wouldn't pay any attention to Him, because He only had three years in the ministry. "Why, I've got thirty-five years in the ministry. You're just a young pup; you don't know anything yet. You need to come up through the ranks like the rest of us."

I might be going out on a limb here, but I'm pretty sure we all can learn from Jesus and how He conducted Himself. To that end, let's look at Jesus in action.

And the third day there was a marriage in Cana of Galilee; and the mother of Jesus was there: and both Jesus was called, and his disciples, to the marriage. And when they wanted wine, the mother of Jesus saith unto him, They have no wine. Jesus saith unto her, Woman, what

have I to do with thee? mine hour is not yet come.

John 2:1-4

Wow! Does He sound like He is walking in love and honoring His mother here? He calls His mama "woman" and says to her in front of everybody, "What have I to do with thee?" She comes to him at this party and tells Him that the host has run out of wine. Never mind that He shouldn't even have been at a party where they were serving alcohol. His attitude towards His mother is not our Sunday school picture of those WWJD bracelets. He's not happy about being bothered with the party logistics and lack of planning.

His mother saith unto the servants, Whatsoever he saith unto you, do it.

John 2:5

They must have had the kind of relationship that Mary could ignore Jesus' question, for she instructs the catering staff to do whatever He tells them to do. She doesn't take "no" for an answer, and she doesn't get offended at His response.

And there were set there six waterpots of stone, after the manner of the purifying of the Jews, containing two or three firkins apiece. Jesus saith unto them, Fill the waterpots with water. And they filled them up to the brim.

John 2:6-7

Remember last chapter when we talked about the mikvah and the cleansing of the hands? These six pots of stone, each holding twenty to thirty gallons each, were there to keep the mikvah full so that folks could keep the law and keep their hands washed. The pots must have been empty, because the whole crowd of party goers were using the mikvah. So Jesus tells the servants to go and fill them up.

And he saith unto them, Draw out now, and bear unto the governor of the feast. And they bare it.

John 2:8

The governor of the feast is the guy in charge of catering the wedding reception; he was probably named Wolfgang. The catering staff takes the water pots, filled with water, to Wolfgang to taste. Can you imagine being one of the catering staff and taking what you know is water to the boss for approval of the wine about to be served? You know how temperamental Wolfgang is about the food and wine; Gordon Ramsey learned everything he knows from this guy. You know that, if this wine isn't really good, you all are getting fired.

When the ruler of the feast had tasted the water that was made wine, and knew not whence it was: (but the servants which drew the water knew;) the governor of the feast called the bridegroom, and saith unto him, Every man at the

beginning doth set forth good wine; and when men have well drunk, then that which is worse: but thou hast kept the good wine until now.

John 2:9-10

I was brought up in church and we were always taught that the wine in the Bible was really grape juice, blah, blah, blah. Well, that's just not the truth. The truth is that the words "well drunk" in the Greek mean intoxicated. Wolfgang compliments the bridegroom for saving the best wine for last after everyone is blitzed and can't tell the difference. I know this fact upsets our religious sensibilities, but everything about the covenant upsets our religious sensibilities. Jesus starts His ministry by making out of water one hundred eighty gallons of the finest wine in world history. Don't you just hate how the Bible and Jesus ruin all of our ideas about Christianity?

This beginning of miracles did Jesus in Cana of Galilee, and manifested forth his

glory; and his disciples believed on him. After this he went down to Capernaum, he, and his mother, and his brethren, and his disciples: and they continued there not many days. And the Jews' Passover was at hand, and Jesus went up to Jerusalem.

John 2:11-13

Let me set up the next part. We know that Jesus missed three Passovers during the time He was in Egypt before Herod died. Luke 2 says that He and His parents went up to Jerusalem every year for Passover. So we know that He's been to the Temple at least twenty-seven times.

Have you ever been to a sporting event in an arena or stadium with all kinds of souvenir stands everywhere? The vendors are selling everything from programs and hotdogs to peanuts and beer. You can't just get to your seats; to get into the arena, you have to pass through the gauntlet of vendors. That kind of scene greets Jesus as He is going into church. This clutter didn't happen overnight; it has been going on a long time.

After twenty-seven years of seeing this circus sideshow of vendors, Jesus comes to church for the first time since He started His ministry.

And found in the temple those that sold oxen and sheep and doves, and the changers of money sitting.

John 2:14

One translation calls these people "loan sharks". People didn't use credit cards back in those days. What the money changers would do is loan money to the people who were coming to make sacrifice to God and get right with Him by pushing back their mistakes and on purposes for another year. I thought Christian television was bad at milking people for money, but these guys were sharking money to people so that they could buy animals to sacrifice that they couldn't afford. Imagine having to borrow money to get right with God.

Most people have this idea of Jesus being "Brother Love, wearing Birkenstocks from the lost tribes of Vermont. He's all about peace and love; He wouldn't do anything to stir up trouble. He certainly wouldn't show His anger. Remember, be ye angry and sin not. No way would Jesus hit anybody."

And when <u>he had made a scourge of small cords</u>, he drove them all out of the temple, and the sheep, and the oxen; and poured out the changers' money, and overthrew the tables; and said unto them that sold doves, Take these things hence; make not my Father's house an house of merchandise.

John 2:15-16

(emphasis mine)

Jesus premeditatedly makes a whip and assaults the vendors and loan sharks. He drives them and their animals out and dumps the furniture and money all over the place. If somebody walked into your church and did all that, he would make the service a little uncomfortable, don't you think? Here Jesus is in church putting on this scene, running folks out, assaulting them with a whip, and dumping over the kiosks.

I'm not feeling the "WWJD bracelet love" here. He's pretty cranked up. When you're overturning furniture and whipping people, you aren't being all nice and sweet and speaking in Shakespearean King James. Walking in love, that's what we're talking about, remember?

And his disciples remembered that it was written, The zeal of thine house hath eaten me up. Then answered the Jews and said unto him, What sign shewest thou unto us, seeing that thou doest these things? Jesus answered and said unto them, Destroy this temple, and in three days I will raise it up. Then said the Jews, Forty and six years was this temple in building, and wilt thou rear it up in three days? But he spake of the temple of his body. When therefore he was risen

from the dead, his disciples remembered that he had said this unto them; and they believed the scripture, and the word which Jesus had said. Now when he was in Jerusalem at the Passover, in the feast day, many believed in <u>his name</u>, when they saw the miracles which he did. But Jesus did not commit himself unto them, because he knew all men, and needed not that any should testify of man: for he knew what was in man.

John 2:17-25

(emphasis mine)

Many believed in His name, and they saw the miracles He did. He worked miracles in the Temple right after He cleaned out the place. Notice the principle here. No wonder we don't see miracles in church today; maybe we would if we just cleaned out all the merchandizing.

Notice that Jesus did not commit trust to men. Love people but don't commit trust to them. Love God and trust God. Love people, but trust God.

Know up front, like Jesus did, that people will let you down. Let's not blame them and judge them; you and I have let people down before and most likely will again. Love people, but place your trust in God. Just because people believe on the name of Jesus doesn't mean they should be trusted. Walking in love does not involve trusting others.

Jesus trusted His disciples and the seventy, those who were faithful and committed. He did not trust those who showed up to His meetings and were involved. My rule of thumb here deals with the chicken and the pig. With your breakfast eggs and bacon, the chicken is involved, but the pig is committed. God never asks for your involvement; He asks for your commitment. Do not commit trust to people who are only involved, and in this way fulfill the new commandment, loving others as Jesus loves us.

Here's the end of His ministry. From the beginning to the end, three years later, we pick up the story on Palm Sunday, one week before Passover, three years after the first time He "walked in love" to the money changers at the Temple.

And the disciples went, and did as Jesus commanded them, and brought the ass, and the colt, and put on them their clothes, and they set him thereon. And a very great multitude spread their garments in the way; others cut down branches from the trees, and strawed them in the way. And the multitudes that went before, and that followed, cried, saying, Hosanna to the son of David: Blessed is he that cometh in the name of the Lord; Hosanna in the highest. And when he was come into Jerusalem, all the city was moved, saying, Who is this? And the multitude said, This is Jesus the prophet of Nazareth of Galilee. And Jesus went into the temple of God, and cast out all them that sold and bought in the temple, and overthrew the tables of the moneychangers, and the seats of them that sold doves, and said unto them, It is written, My house shall be called the house of prayer; but ye have made it a

den of thieves. And the blind and the lame came to him in the temple; and he healed them.

Matthew 21:6-14

There goes Brother Love again, turning over the furniture and running off the vendors during church. Last time, they asked for a sign to prove authority. This time He doesn't wait for the challenge and just begins to heal people in church.

And when the chief priests and scribes saw the wonderful things that he did, and the children crying in the temple, and saying, Hosanna to the son of David; they were sore displeased, and said unto him, Hearest thou what these say? And Jesus saith unto them, Yea; <u>have ye never read</u>, Out of the mouth of babes and sucklings thou hast perfected praise?

Matthew 21:15-16

(emphasis mine)

Jesus is being extremely sarcastic with the priests and scribes here. *No, Andrew, Jesus would never be sarcastic; that's a sin, isn't it?* These guys not only read the law, they memorized the whole thing, all five books of the law (Genesis, Exodus, Leviticus, Numbers, and Deuteronomy). Jesus asks them, "Have ye never read?" That's like asking a surgeon, "Have you ever heard of a scalpel?"

Wait a minute, what He said doesn't sound like the "WWJD bracelet-turn-the-other-cheek" Jesus I heard about in church. He spices the gumbo with a sarcastic quip and then walks out and leaves. Let me ask a few questions. Did Jesus love the chief priests and scribes? Did Jesus love the money changers and vendors? Did Jesus forgive them? Did they ask for forgiveness?

Do you remember the guy whose friends let him down through the roof to see Jesus? He wanted to get healed, and Jesus said, "Your sins are forgiven." Did that guy ask for his sins to be forgiven? NO! He wanted healing, not forgiveness.

How about the lady everybody wanted to stone that was caught committing adultery? Jesus asked, "Where are your accusers?" She said she didn't know and that no man was left to condemn her. Jesus said, "I don't condemn you, either. Go and sin no more." Did she ask for forgiveness? NO! She just didn't want to get stoned to death. Jesus forgave her.

What about the Roman soldiers, those guys who nailed Him to the cross and then played rock, paper, scissors to see who got His jacket? Jesus said, "Father forgive them, for they know not what they do." Did they ask for forgiveness? Did He love them?

Jesus forgives everybody, whether they ask for forgiveness or not. He loves everybody, whether they want His love or not. Did the fact that He loves them keep Him from letting the money changers and chief priests and scribes from being jerks in His presence? NO! He did not allow them to keep being idiots in His presence and hurting other people. Jesus is showing us how to walk in love. You can love people and forgive people and at the same time stop their nonsense.

If somebody is hurting other people and you stop him, are you walking in love? According to Jesus' actions, you are. If somebody is hurting one of my church members, and I don't stop it because I don't want to be confrontational and mean as a pastor and so I tell everybody, "Let's all just turn the other cheek," am I walking in love? NO! Turning the other cheek means that bad folks get the benefit of the doubt and get one free hit. Jesus never told us to keep turning cheeks; He said turn one time.

I get so sick of seeing Christians just watch as their brothers and sisters get hammered in the world. That passivity is not walking in love. If you can't stop someone from hurting others, you are not fulfilling the new commandment. The Ten Commandments will allow you to cower in corner and let others get hurt. Loving others the way Jesus loves us will not allow you to duck and hide while others are destroyed.

The book of Revelation records the last words Jesus spoke to the church, i.e. us. He describes how He loves us, and His words don't jive with the WWJD message purveyed in churches today.

Those whom I [dearly and tenderly] love, I tell their faults and convict and convince and reprove and chasten [I discipline and instruct them]. So be enthusiastic and in earnest and burning with zeal and repent [changing your mind and attitude].

Revelation 3:19 (AMP)

He says whom I love I tell their faults. Did He do something about all those faults that He saw going on in the Temple? He did in a big way. Notice about Jesus that He tenderly corrected the woman at the well in Samaria her faults, but He hammered the religious leaders publicly and in a big way. We should be aware of how correction will be received. If people's hearts are receptive, don't hammer them, but if people are intent on hurting others for their own gain, hammer them. Don't get upset; we're just reading the Bible.

All my life, I was brought up in church and taught that this next verse is a verse on "salvation". This verse is NOT a verse on salvation. Jesus is talking about walking in love towards people, people whom He just finished telling their faults.

Behold, I stand at the door and knock; if anyone hears and listens to and heeds My voice and opens the door, I will come in to him and will eat with him, and he [will eat] with Me.

Revelation 3:20 (AMP)

This verse isn't talking about salvation. He's saying, "After I tell you your faults and make you quit being a jerk and stop you from hurting others, I'll stand here and make restoration available. Our relationship can go forward anytime you want it to, because I'm right here for you. If you need my help, I'm right here for you. I'm at the door, and I'm waiting for you."

Walking in love requires us to protect others from harm, but it also requires that we leave the door open for restoration to those we have to stop from doing harm to others. Walking in love allows no room for grudges or bitterness toward others. We aren't called to make others do the right thing but merely stop them from hurting others. Jesus never made the money changers or priests and scribes do the right thing; what He did was stop them from doing the wrong thing in His presence. They went right back to doing the wrong thing after He left the Temple.

We aren't to go around trying to make people do the right thing; we are to stop others from being hurt in our presence, though. I hope you can see the difference. God never makes anyone do the right thing. Think about your own life; does He make you write out a tithe check? Does He make you speak only good things over your life? Does He make you live in blessing (consistently lucky success)? No, and we shouldn't either; using force is not fulfilling the new commandment. Stopping others from being hurt is fulfilling the new commandment.

The Love of Christ

In the entire Bible, the term "the love of Christ" appears only three times. The Bible frequently references "the love of God", but not so often "the love of Christ". I want to look at all three of those references and see what other clues they give us to fulfilling the new commandment to love one another as Jesus loves us.

For the love of Christ constraineth us; because we thus judge, that if one died for all, then were all dead.

2 Corinthians 5:14

The love of Christ constrains us. What does that phrase mean? In the Greek, constraineth literally means to hold something together lest it fall apart to pieces. The love of Christ will help keep us together lest we fall to pieces. A guy in our church, we'll call him Baby Brother, gave me permission to tell this story, which illustrates how this principle applies to real life in real time.

This story is about Baby Brother and Big Brother. Big Brother, just out of prison, restarts his deck and fence company. The brothers are on a job when Big Brother gets into an argument with one of his laborers. The feud quickly degenerates into fisticuffs, and Big Brother is so enraged that he begins to fall to pieces, beating the laborer to a pulp. Baby Brother realizes that Big Brother is going to go right back to prison if he doesn't constrain him from really hurting the laborer. Baby Brother places himself between the two combatants and tells the laborer to run. At this point, Big Brother is really mad and starts whaling on Baby Brother. One of them gets a brand new set of broken ribs and the other receives the gift of black eyes, and both end up in the emergency room.

Baby Brother loved Big Brother the way that Christ loves us, on many different levels, but we're talking about "constrained". Baby Brother put himself in the middle of the fight to keep Big Brother from falling to pieces and ending up back in the slammer. Baby Brother pictures what the love of Christ does for us, in the middle of one of life's crises; His love holds us together lest we fall apart. Baby Brother fulfilled the new commandment by placing himself in the middle of Big Brother's crisis. If the power lies in our hand to do so, we need to help our brothers and sisters to keep themselves together lest they fall to pieces.

The next reference of "the love of Christ" I want to look at appears in the middle of the Ephesians prayer that we went over earlier in this chapter.

That Christ may dwell in your hearts by faith; that ye, being rooted and grounded in love, may be able to comprehend with all saints what is the breadth, and length, and depth, and height; and <u>to know the love of Christ, which passeth knowledge</u>, that ye might be filled with all the fulness of God.

Ephesians 3:17-19

(emphasis mine)

The Greek sheds some light on the King James English here. In the original language the phrase "which passeth knowledge" literally means that "you can only know by practical experience". This phrase is so true. You can read about the love of Christ and hear about the love of Christ and gather information (knowledge) about the love of Christ, but until you yourself experience the love of Christ in real life and real time, the knowledge means nothing.

So praying this prayer for yourself and for others, that we would have practical experience of the love of Christ, is so important. Notice the byproduct of experiencing the love of Christ practically: that you might be filled with all the fullness of God. WOW! If we believers were filled with all the fullness of God, look out! Your life would be running on all eight cylinders and turbo-charged. Does God have life? Is God in a position of honor? Docs God have riches? God has riches, honor, and life, and when you experience on a practical level the love of Christ, you will begin to be filled with the fullness of God. With that fullness we receive the benefits of the covenant: riches, honor, and life.

Fulfilling the new commandment releases the byproduct of riches, honor, and life. We are not to make getting those things our focus. If we focus on loving one another as Christ loves us, the aftereffect is riches, honor and life. As a Marine infantryman and a cop and a federal agent, I had to qualify with various firearms. The principles of marksmanship are simple and productive if applied. One must focus on the front site post, not the target. The human eye can only focus on one thing at a time. Most people focus on the target so that the front site post becomes blurry, and their shots are off. If you focus on the front site post (the new commandment) and the target is blurry (riches, honor, and life), your aim will be true, and you will hit the target.

Interestingly enough, the word "sin" literally means in the original languages "to miss the target", and it was taken from a word in an archery contest. When contestants missed the mark or target, they sinned. Anything less than God's perfect will for us is "sin" or missing the target. If we live in less than riches, honor, and life, the benefits of the covenant which Jesus bought with His blood, we are sinning, missing the target. Focus not on the religious traditions of the law and Ten Commandments, trying to measure up and do "good", but rather focus on the practical experience of loving one another as Jesus loves us. Then you will begin to hit the target on a regular basis.

This chapter includes many real world practical applications in fulfilling the new commandment. Reread this chapter and grab a notepad to jot down some ways in which you can incorporate them into your life so that you can begin to experience the benefits of this very expensive covenant God has provided for us.

The final reference of "the love of Christ" is in the book of Romans, and it is very powerful, which is why I saved it for last.

Who shall separate us from the love of Christ? shall tribulation, or distress, or persecution, or famine, or nakedness, or peril, or sword? As it is written, For thy

**sake we are killed all the day long; we
are accounted as sheep for the slaughter.**

Romans 8:35-36

I've heard preachers say, "It is written that we
are killed all day long for Jesus. We're just sheep
to the slaughter for the Lord. It's an honor and a
privileged to suffer for Him." The very next word
out of the apostle Paul's mouth is...NO!

**<u>Nay</u>, in all these things <u>we are more than
conquerors</u> through him that loved us.**

Romans 8:37

(emphasis mine)

We are more than conquerors. A conqueror is a
championship MMA fighter who goes five rounds
with the world's best, takes a beating, but wins in
the end. That guy's wife is more than a conqueror
when the champ goes home and hands her the
purse for the fight. That's us; we're more than conquerors. Jesus wins the fight and then hands us

the purse for the fight, containing riches, honor, and life.

For I am persuaded, that neither death, nor life, nor angels, nor principalities, nor powers, nor things present, nor things to come, nor height, nor depth, nor any other creature, shall be able to separate us from the love of God, which is in Christ Jesus our Lord.

Romans 8:38-39

His love for us acts in this manner; He won't cut and run on you in a fight. When I was a street cop, I gauged my partners by one standard: Would this guy or girl leave me if we had to fight bad guys? In all my years in law enforcement, I only had three partners that wouldn't leave me in a fight. You can overlook a lot of shortcomings in a person who doesn't leave you when things get really rough. I didn't care what kind of cologne they wore, what their quirks were, or if they spit on you when they talked; if they would stick with me in a fight for my life and not cut and run, they were good cops.

Did you notice that all the things listed here that won't separate us from His love are all part of the dark side of the law, the curse of the law? Poverty, dishonor, nakedness, peril, shame, death, the sword, sickness, and famine: each of these is part of the curse of the law. I love the fact that Jesus will never cut and run on me, even in the middle of the worst possible circumstances. If you find yourself in the middle of the dark side, take inventory. Are you trying to keep the law, trying to keep your religious tradition? *(And every denomination and non-denomination has its own tradition(s) for its people to keep; that's why they split off.)* Dump the tradition and take up the new commandment, the love of Christ, and you become more than a conqueror.

In fulfilling the new commandment, to love one another as Jesus loves us, we shouldn't cut and run on our brothers and sisters, either. I see this weakness all the time in churches. When somebody goes through something, somebody fails, gets into adultery, gets cancer, goes through a divorce, or their kids die in a car accident, we "Christians" cut and run on them. We don't want to get involved. We have our own issues. We're really busy. We're not emotionally available to handle their trauma, etc., etc., and on and on. Then we wonder why no one comes to help us in our time of need. When somebody is hurting, when they're in shame, just lost their job or the house or the car, when they don't have enough provision, when they are in sickness, or they are having a hard time in relationships, don't leave them in a fight. Jesus never leaves us; no matter how bad things are, He doesn't leave us in a fight. We shouldn't leave each other in a fight, either. After all, we are all in this covenant together: God, Jesus, Abraham, you, me, and everyone in between that has placed his faith in Christ.

Final Word

I encourage you to reread this book several times and let the ideas sink in. Mediate on the truths and Scriptures contained in it. I know some of the teaching goes against the grain of our religious upbringing. Search each Scripture out for yourself; don't take my word for what it says. If you have a computer and Internet access, download www.e-sword.net. It's free, and it comes with the original languages of both the Old and New Testaments. Scroll over the number next to each English word, and the Greek or Hebrew word and meaning will pop up.

The Bible is a legal document; it is your covenant. Don't ever take a preacher's or minister's word for what belongs to you. Search the truth out for yourself. The sad fact is that most ministers are only regurgitating what they heard from their ministers, teachers, and professors at Bible college or seminary.

If you only remember three words from this book, I'll have done my job. Remember that your covenant is summed in the three words RICHES, HONOR, and LIFE. Run everything in your life through the filter of these three words. If something shows up in your life that doesn't fit into one of these three categories, riches, honor, and life, then dump it. It's not part of your covenant, and it didn't come from God.

Covenant for Rookies

> **By humility [believe and act like God's smarter than you] and the fear of the LORD [to hate evil: adversity, affliction, calamity, displeasure, distress (WORRY), exceeding great grief, harm, heaviness, hurt, ill favor, misery, sadness, sorrow, trouble, and wrong like a personal enemy] are riches, and honor, and life.**
>
> **Proverbs 22:4**
> **(emphasis mine)**

Benediction

As I said, we all have our traditions, and one of mine is to close every service by putting us in remembrance of our covenant. I wrote this prayer for my firstborn. All of my kids have heard these words prayed over them from before birth until they could pray it themselves and do so every night before bed. I'd like to close this book by putting us all in remembrance of our covenant.

Father, I thank You for Your Word; I thank You that it's true and that it works in my life all the time, even when I'm not looking.

Thank You for supreme intelligence and skill and the mind of Christ.

Thank You for divine health and healing.

Thank You for supernatural protection and supernatural prosperity.

Thank You for supernatural uncommon favor with men and women everywhere looking to give to us.

In Jesus' mighty name I pray, Amen.

May God bless you with riches, honor, and life in the covenant,

Andrew

LaVergne, TN USA
25 May 2010
183836LV00007B/4/P